Dedication

To my wife Claudia for her encouraging counsel and
inspiration, 17 years of wonderful marriage and her
many hours of typing;

To Howard Flaherty, executive producer of the *Fantasy
Explosion* video, fellow adventurer and friend;

To Gabe Arosemena for his ideas, typing and friendship;

To Winkie Pratney, whose insight into God's Word and our
culture birthed the idea for this book;

To Tony Salerno and the Agape Force for their faith in me
and in my dreams;

To Rich Wilkerson, Tim LaHaye and Dawson McAllister
for their comments and appearances in the companion
video to this book; and

Most of all, to our Lord Jesus Christ, who gave me the
dream to write this book and the grace to stay with it
until it was finished.

Contents

Foreword

The raw nerves of a culture bombarded by media manipulation and sexual exploitation are being salved with the superficial. Bob Maddux is doing a lot of people a favor, helping them confront the deception of the fantastic.

I feel the apostle Paul would step into most homes today and shout again the mandate declared to the Corinthians ages ago: Cast down imaginations—they boast themselves against God. Bring your thoughts into obedience to Jesus! (See 2 Cor. 10:5.)

Bob has captured that message and applied it with relevancy to our present moment. Tune in. Here's something *real*.

Jack W. Hayford

Preface
Living the Fantasy

In Houston, Texas, thousands of parents and their children are regular visitors to a new amusement game known as *Photon*. This computer-coordinated, interactive game offers clientele the illusion of being in a fantasy world of wonder and action. The players, dressed in space-age clothing, and firing realistic laser-like weapons, have each paid $3.50 to enter the elaborate space-age battlefield housed in a 10,000 square-foot building.[1]

In Cape May, New Jersey, a group of 50 people gather for a weekend of murder and mystery. A company known as *Murder to Go, Inc.* organizes the players and eight actors into a game of whodunit. The goal is to solve a make-believe crime in the tradition of mystery writer Agatha Christie. The murder weekenders have each paid $300 to participate in this excursion into mystery fantasy.[2]

In a densely wooded forest a group of grown men in army-type camouflage, their faces smeared with black grease paint, blend into the scenery in a game of outfoxing

9

and outgunning their opponents. They're playing the *National Survival Game*. Instead of being armed with real weapons and live ammunition, they carry marking guns that shoot paint pellets: one splatter of paint and you're dead! Although it's all a game, the fighting is intense, and triumph brings exultation. To see grown men playing this game would seem almost humorous if not for the fact that they appear unreasonably obsessed with a make-believe world.

In Chicago, the audience at a stage production called *Dungeon Master* not only watches the actors but becomes part of the play. "Characters" selected at random from the audience, dressed in homemade costumes complete with mock swords, shields, axes and armor, join in the dramas. For pre-teen Dragon fans, there is a special weekly children's show that allows them the opportunity to act out their own fantasy roles.[3]

Events like these take place every day in cities and towns scattered across our nation. They affect youth and adults alike. What do all these occurrences have in common? Perhaps they are evidence of a new phenomenon. America is in the throws of a new era, the era of "fan-diction" (addiction to fantasy). Many of these fads are more than imaginary mental escapes. Often they are active attempts to live out a dream.

Maybe the increasing pressures of modern life have created this strange desire to run away from reality. It seems people want a total escape. They desire to step into another world completely, shrugging off the problems of their present struggles. If one's not loved and accepted in this life, they can always become an admired hero in a make-believe world. Like Walter Mitty, the fictional character who escaped the humdrum of his dreary life by winning imaginary airplane battles, people chase after these illusions to ease the pain of boredom. The only difference with many in

10

this new generation is that they are not content to keep these fantasies inside their heads.

Are some of these escapes harmful? A closer look may bring some interesting conclusions. It's possible that modern man is hooked on a new "drug." One that's easy to get. A fix that's as close as one's mind. But can the improper use of fantasy wound us and cause lasting scars?

Understanding the mind's power and the effects media is having on us is the first focus of this book. The second is on the practical steps we can take in dealing with these images while allowing God to unlock in us the kind of visions that will catch us up in His wonder.

1
Dreams

They're What We're Made Of

The human mind is fascinating and powerful. It stores and processes information, and at the same time is constantly developing ideas. The ideas that flow from the imagination can in turn mold our lives and shape our futures. A good illustration of this is the story of Heinrich Schliemann and his search for the mythological city of Troy.

In 1831 Heinrich's father gave his seven-year-old son a Christmas present that changed his life, and added a chapter to the history of archeology. The gift was an illustrated book containing a picture of the city of Troy in flames. At that time, most historians felt that Troy was merely a literary invention of Homer, the ancient Greek poet. Yet this picture so fired the imagination of young Heinrich that he was determined to discover the city.

Decades later, after years of hard work and research, Schliemann unearthed the reality of what he had searched for. Digging in the ancient ruins of a large mound of earth located in Turkey, he discovered artifacts of Troy hidden for thousands of years. His dream had come true.

The treasures unearthed at the ruins of Homeric Troy are a magnificent testimony to a man who followed his dream and saw it come true. But there can be danger in this realm as well. Someone once said that our generation is like Joseph: We're dreamers. Yet, unlike Joseph, the dreams we pursue are often our own, and not the ones given to us by God. Through history, both biblical and secular, we have seen men chase after dreams and find them.

In the early chapters of the book of Genesis we see the account of the building of the tower of Babel (see Gen. 11:1-6). This massive project was undertaken by a civilization that possessed a common vision. They dreamed of building a tower whose peak would reach into the heavens. This group effort was an attempt to defy God's purpose for mankind. God recognized that if this effort was not stopped soon the power of man's unrestrained and rebellious imagination would be released.

The united efforts on the tower were not nearly as dangerous as the united dreams. God understood that wicked men with wicked dreams would seek to live out their dreams. If they were not stopped, then "nothing will be restrained from them, which they have imagined to do" (Gen. 11:6). God halted the construction of the tower and scattered man over the face of the earth.

A modern-day example of men seeking to live out their evil dreams took place not too long ago right here in America. A newspaper article told of a neo-Nazi group that used as their "bible" the fictional novel entitled *The Turner Diaries*. This book was used as the group's guide as they allegedly committed violent crimes throughout the West. Apparently, they were not content to merely fantasize about a Nazi

14

plot; they wanted to see it become reality. Although this story is a unique one, it illustrates the power of imagination to mold our real lives.[1]

Explosive Multiplication

I remember as a child watching a demonstration used to explain how a nuclear explosion takes place. A room was filled with mousetraps, set and carefully placed side by side until the floor was completely covered. A Ping-Pong ball was then placed on each trap. What followed was an amazing sight. A single ball was tossed into the room. When it landed, it triggered off one of the traps and now two balls were airborne. These landed and four shot up into the air. In a matter of seconds, there was an explosion of Ping-Pong balls, as the principle of multiplication took over.

The First Fantasy Explosion

So it was with the first fantasy explosion. When God created man, He created him with a pure mind. All of man's thoughts dwelt on the wonder of God and His creation. Yet into this state of innocence was injected a single vain imagination. It started out with the lie Satan told Eve, "You will not surely die . . . you will be like God" (Gen. 3:4,5, *NIV*). This first spark of evil soon escalated into a nightmare of wickedness and perversion that saturated the earth. God had to take action:

> And God saw that the wickedness of man *was* great in the earth, and *that* every imagination of the thoughts of his heart *was* only evil continually (Gen. 6:5).

This eruption of perverted thinking eventually resulted

in the destruction of all of mankind, with the exception of Noah and his family

Today's Fantasy Explosion

Where do our dreams and fantasies come from today? Perhaps the most prolific source is the media. Films, TV, magazines and music groups create images in our minds that mold not only our way of thinking, but also our actions. In interviews with young people, we asked them if they had ever seen the clone of a famous rock star. They knew immediately what we were talking about. They had all seen someone who dressed and acted like their rock-star hero. All of us, at one time or another, have had someone we admire and want to be like. Biblically, we can see that Jesus and the apostles are role models for Christians. But what happens when our role models are faulty and our dream is a deception?

Frequently, modern man chooses role models who come from the realm of fantasy. Today's heroes are invented by Hollywood and the image brokers on Madison Avenue. In his book, *The TV Ritual: Worship at the Video Altar*, Gregor T. Goethals makes the observation that there are two dimensions on which TV works. One level informs, sells products and entertains. But, he points out, there is a more pervasive realm in which TV functions:

> All television images—news, sports, sitcoms, commercials, soap operas—provide the American public with fundamental rituals and myths. Much of what people think about the "good life," the roles of men and women, technology, or the changing patterns of family and political life, emerge from the television set.[2]

With 90 million American households watching TV each night, you wonder what effect the harmless-looking cathode-ray tube is having.

Whether or not the media has the power to shape our lives has long been a hotly disputed issue. Government studies seem to reinforce the concept that certain kinds of media images can have a negative influence on society. A *New York Times* article tells us:

> A federal analysis of a decade's research on the behavioral effects of television viewing has concluded that there is now "overwhelming" scientific evidence [that] "excessive" violence on television leads directly to aggressive and violent behavior among children and teenagers.[3]

Violence is only one of many areas of concern. Decadence can begin in the corrupt mind of a TV scriptwriter and become such alluring imagery on the screen that it creates not only new heroes, but different values and life-styles.

The Rocky Horror Picture Show is just one of many glaring examples of how imagery on the screen influences the behavior and life-styles of viewers. Although somewhat passé now, in its heyday it was a graphic illustration of the effect of fantasy on behavior. At one time, 230 independent film houses across the United States gave weekly showings of this perverted and bizarre movie involving science fiction and cabaret-style sexuality.

As if the film isn't weird enough in itself, what goes on in front of the screen is even stranger. Many of those who attend this weekly event (some have seen it over 100 times) mimic and act out the scenario portrayed on the screen. Others who attend dress themselves like the debauched characters who are the heroes of the film, and repeatedly talk back to the images flickering on the screen in front of them.

What does all this unusual behavior say about our generation? Is there some ultimate design behind the effect fantasy in the media is having on our world?

In the following chapters we will investigate many of the major factors surrounding this controversial issue, and point out the dangers as well as biblical mandates and alternatives available for a generation hooked on a deadly dream.

TAKING INVENTORY

Films, TV, magazines and *music* make up a large part of the media that is having an effect on us today. Whether or not we realize it, we are being influenced by what we see and hear through the agencies of mass communication. Let's take a look at the four areas listed above and see what part these play in the lives of you and your family:

1. *Films* - How often do your family members go to the movies or rent movies for your VCR? List the last five films you and/or your family members viewed.

2. *TV* - On an average, how many hours a week is your TV viewed? List your family's favorite TV shows.

3. *Magazines* - To what magazines do you regularly subscribe? List those periodicals currently in your home.

4. *Music* - List the different types of music representative of your household. How often do you purchase record albums or tapes? Do you listen to the radio on a regular basis?

What kinds of influences (positive or negative) could these forms of media have on your life and the lives of your family members? Discuss each of the areas above separately.

2
Contemporary Music
Rock, Pop and Videos

The sound is overwhelming. The rhythm of the music pounds into the audience like a velvet-covered pile driver. The air is heavy with the smell of sweaty bodies. The thousands of people in the audience are on their feet, many with hands in the air, shouting out the lyrics along with the singers on stage. Suddenly, just as the music reaches the right decibel, a girl clad in a G-string is tied to a torture rack; a black hood is put over her head. Then one of the band members pretends to beat her on the head. Fake blood flows over her body as he attacks her.[1]

Is this a scene from hell? Is it some bizarre segment from an X-rated movie? No, it's a concert by one of the latest, and most grotesque-looking, heavy-metal rock groups around today.

When the rock star walks on stage, near-worshipful clapping and shouting fill the large exhibition hall. He is clad in the most outrageous clothing his costume designers can create. A female member of his group, naked from the waist up, slithers onto the stage. Reaching down, she pulls a fan from the audience onto the stage, and then in front of everyone begins passionate lovemaking. As the concert continues, the musical lyrics graphically describe a vivid array of sexual activities.[2]

Secular music has long been one of the main vehicles for fantasy. Its cunning and seductive sounds bypass inhibitions and carries its message straight to the heart. The crowds streaming from a super-star, super-charged concert can live for weeks on the emotional high such an ecstatic experience brings. The images and sounds they've seen and heard will leave impressions that last a lifetime. Yet are these the type of memories that make for stable lives and happy marriages, or do they stir the kind of passions that only adultery and fornication can satisfy?

If these concerts were not enough to cause us concern, what about the ongoing assault on this generation that pours forth from millions of stereos, AM/FM radios and clothing store sound systems. Modern youth hardly have a quiet moment for reflection. This is the generation that has made music one of its main courses in a banquet of hedonistic pleasures.

Music Is the Fantasy

Today, more and more young people discover and express their fantasies through music. A recent TV show, "Putting on the Hits," has the contestants dress up like their favorite rock star and then lip sync the lyrics to the sound track. Sing-along parties where party goers become the "stars" as they sing along with the latest pop songs are becoming more and more popular. As one commentator put it, "It doesn't so much matter whether you can sing well or not, or even if the person performing the song can sing well.

21

It's the experience of being that person, identifying with what they're saying through the lyrics, and then trying to live out what's been sung about that's important."

All of this would not be nearly as dangerous if it weren't for the fact that much of what's being portrayed through secular music today is immoral and selfish, if not totally depraved. Parents who were shocked 25 years ago with the wild antics of Elvis Presley or the Beatles would be totally devastated if they took the time to listen to one of their teenager's records, or attend a rock concert by Prince or Madonna. Susan Baker, wife of the Treasury Secretary, made this observation:

> Some of these lyrics reinforce all the wrong kinds
> of values for children at a very tender age. For
> many adults, the beat of such songs is so heavy
> and the words so indistinguishable that it takes a
> while to catch on. One of my friends had been
> exercising to this music for hours before she
> became aware of the lyrics.[3]

Certainly not all of secular music can be classified in the same category, but the predominant trend is one of frightening sensuality and godless philosophy.

The Lyrics

A Russian Communist leader once stated that with 26 little soldiers (the letters of the alphabet), he could conquer the world. He understood the power of the written word. Yet in the closing years of the twentieth century, there appears to be an even more powerful force for conquering lives, that is, the spoken (sung) word linked with the magic of contemporary music.

Anyone who's found themselves in the middle of their morning shower singing the lyrics to a fast-food restaurant's jingle knows the power music has to make words stick in our minds to be repeated over and over again. After a while it can be annoying if not a bit humorous. It can also mean big bucks for the hamburger chain whose name is remembered. The problem with the "jingles" of most secular music is that they're not selling hamburgers.

The lyrics of today's minstrels have come a long way from the innocent songs of a generation ago. Modern music has stepped over the line of decency and its message has become laced with graphic descriptions of sexual activity.

Sexual Perversion

In the fall of 1985, Capital Hill was ablaze in a controversy with a new twist. The wives of top government officials were upset. In their concern, they were trying to bring the record industry and artists to task over the apparent spread of illicit and pornographic lyrics on many of today's popular record albums. They were concerned and had a right to be. The wives paraded by a congressional committee a display of "X-rated" songs, whose lyrics make even grownups blush. These words have become common knowledge to millions of American teens.

The now tame lyrics of Mick Jagger singing, "Let's Spend the Night Together" have given way to the likes of "Sugar Walls," a song clearly reveling in genital arousal. And songs like "Darling Nikki" by Prince leave little to the imagination with lyrics that talk about a girl named Nikki, a sex fiend he meets in a hotel lobby masturbating with a magazine.[4]

Some might suggest that these songs are only samples of fringe artists, yet no one will deny the popularity of

23

Madonna, who on her triple platinum album, "Like a Virgin," sings "Feels So Good Inside."

"Relax When You Want to Come" is a number made popular by an English group, Frankie Goes to Hollywood. Their album, "Relax," in the fall of '85 was the fourth best-selling record in the history of the British music industry. Sadly, these are representative of the milder songs in that genre.

Heavy Metal Goes a Step Farther

Heavy-metal groups take their listeners even farther out. One group, Judas Priest, on their album, "Defenders of the Faith," sing "Eat Me Alive," the words depicting a girl being forced at gunpoint to commit oral sex. Even more explicit are the words of songs by groups like W.A.S.P. For example, the lyrics of one of their songs speaks of pictures of naked ladies lying on the bed and the smell of sweet convulsion and about howling in heat and finally, about committing the sex act, like a beast.[5]

Other unsettling items include blatant occult songs like Grim Reaper's "See You in Hell," a song glorifying satanism.[6]

Sexually explicit lyrics have shocked even record industry professionals. Paul Grein, editor of *Billboard* magazine, commented to one reporter regarding "Erotic City," a Prince song with repeated references to the sex act:

> When I heard "Erotic City" I couldn't believe it.
> After some years in the business, you come to
> think that there are certain absolutes. The fact
> that you could not say this on the radio was cer-
> tainly one of them.[7]

Yet "Erotic City" has had frequent airplay on a variety of radio stations.

The words to these songs do more than entertain; they indoctrinate. Madison Avenue has known for years that a product sells better if the promotion is put to music.

Promotional songs are written with a built-in "musical hook." Long after the ad has first been heard, the message keeps repeating itself in the mind. For some of the youth who have heard the message of today's pop music, the words are having an effect. Youth workers, school leaders and drug abuse counselors sadly report stories of music's power in molding the actions of many of those they deal with.

The Middle of the Road Is Just as Bad

Rock music is not the only segment of the music industry that is turning out immoral messages through its songs. Adults would do well to turn a deaf ear to the "middle of the road" singer who croons about adulterous one-night stands, or the country and western tunes that glorify cheating on your mate and rebelling against authority.

Often it's the subtle, smooth sound of a velvet voice that has encouraged a wife struggling in her mind with adulterous fantasies to carry them out. More than once this author has heard firsthand accounts of married people who have been strongly influenced to walk away from their mates by the romantic melodies and lyrics of a gentle pop song.

At a time in history when there is such a barrage of temptations, why would anyone want to add to them by tuning into a steady stream of sensuous "pablum" that only increases the pressures to run away from one's responsibilities to the fantasy land of mental adultery?

Performers' Life-styles Set a Pattern

Just as influential as the lyrics of their songs are the life-styles of the performers. Teen rock magazines with full-color pictures glorify the lives of these "rock gods." Their pages are full of vivid accounts of the musical stars' living habits. "My bottle of Jack Daniels is my best friend in the world," boasts Nikki Sixx in one interview.[8] In another, he boldly states, "People think we're wild and crazy all the time. Well, they're right . . . we go through women like most people go through socks."[9]

Newspaper and magazine articles on these "heroes of hedonism" abound, giving the graphic details of the rebellious and depraved actions many of them carry out daily. Trashing hotel rooms, ripping things up and biting people until their victims are black and blue is just one account reported in one periodical.[10]

Yet if one continues to wonder what influence these rock stars have on their followers, just ask them, as some Texas disc jockeys did to those of Motley Crue. They asked the band's devoted followers what they would do to go backstage and meet the bandsmen.

One 15-year-old girl said she'd get on her hands and knees and give them her body, and even tear her clothes off if she had to. A 13-year-old girl said, "I'd do it with the Crue till black and blue is all you can see." Another 15-year-old girl said she'd have sex with the ugliest, fattest, most disgusting guy in the world and then she'd even give up her boyfriend by sleeping with his best friend, just to meet the band.

One 13-year-old claimed she'd leave her breast to Motley Crue. The accounts go on with others offering money, bodies and even one youth offering his mother.[11]

Reinforcing the evidence of the negative influence of

these musical groups, Gregory Bodenhamer, who operates an anti-gang program for the Los Angeles County Probation Dept., claims that "80 percent of kids who assault their parents are 'devoted followers' of heavy-metal and punk music."[12] The *Los Angeles Times* stated that he "warns parents that five Orange County teenagers who killed their parents in the past two years were involved with punk and heavy metal."[13]

A steady diet of idolizing and worshiping these musical stars can create in people's minds the desire to imitate the life-styles of their idols. The fantasy can start out as a playful diversion with youth dressing and talking like their role models. "The lyrics of heavy metal, coupled with the costumes and world view of the bands tell kids that it's OK to do whatever you want to do, sex, drugs and rock and roll," Bodenhamer went on to claim.[14]

Another clear example of the negative molding power of pop idols are the recent claims by a child-pornography expert. In a report to the United Press International, Judith Reisman said the following:

> Pictures encourage child pornography. You're dealing with an idol or heroine who carries with her a great deal of power and symbolism. For example, Madonna is seen as a desired being in society, so all young women want to be desired; they want to achieve. If the nude pictures are described in popular magazines as appropriate, desirable behavior, then youngsters, both girls and boys, will construe that to be the case. Large numbers of them will. Thus the pictures will encourage voluntary displays by youngsters. That is not good.[15]

Once again it's the fantasy aspect that plays on the minds of youth. Daydreaming about one's heroes and their actions can begin to produce not only the desire to act out fantasy, but also the actual occurrence as is witnessed by the visual testimony of thousands of "Wanna bees," young girls who dress and talk and act as much like their idols as they possibly can. Will they also step over the line into sexual promiscuity as some experts predict?

Psychologists have known for years the power of music to affect our mental attitudes and emotions. A marketing professor at Loyola University discovered in a study of retail store music that even the background melodies can affect shoppers' moods and increase sales. Restaurants use mood music to increase the patience of waiting customers. Manufacturers have found that they can actually "program" their workers for greater efficiency.[16]

If, as the researchers say, positive music can manipulate us positively, then it's also possible that the negative images projected through much secular music can mold the lives of the listeners in a destructive way. Yet with all the concern over music's influential power on youth now a new force has arisen that may possibly be an even greater molder of minds· music videos.

Music Videos

"Music video sells fantasy. Fantasy in turn sells records."[17] With those words, *Newsweek* magazine opens a brief report in its March '85 issue on women in music videos. It's perhaps just this aspect of fantasy, both visual and audio, that has come together to make this new industry so successful.

MTV, the music video channel, is reported to now be

reaching over 17½ million households.[18] Besides MTV, it is estimated there are approximately 200 programs across the country that show only rock videos.[19]

Some researchers suspect that this growing fad will fade the same way the video game phenomenon has faded, but other studies contradict this. Coleman Research, a media-consulting firm based in Dallas, discovered that the popularity of these videos are producing both new and seasoned viewers. These researchers also found that people can watch videos over and over again without tiring of them. In fact 72 percent who repeatedly watch either enjoy them as much or more than when they first started viewing them. Younger teens even tend to spend more time watching than the older ones.

Coleman's study also found that later on when they hear clips of the songs they've seen on a music video playing on the radio, they "play back" those same video images in their mind.[20] It seems like this kind of reinforcement could have a gripping effect on the viewer/listener's thought life, especially if what they're seeing and hearing is questionable. One rock video executive made the following observation: "Kids around 18 use music to define their identity the way people in middle age use cars and homes."[21] With today's youth defining their identity through music, one asks what kind of identity can they find in the latest outpouring of musical images?

Violence in Rock Videos

For years, violence has been a great part of rock music. The National Coalition on Television Violence states that the violence contained in rock lyrics over the past 20 years has increased 115 percent. Add to this the fact they also found rock videos three times more violent than the record albums themselves.[22] Sometimes it's not the lyrics that are violent at all but the action portrayed on the screen while the music plays. For example, Billy Idol's "Dancing with Myself" features a naked woman with chains on her wrists and a rope around her neck. One magazine commentator pointed out that the group Def Leppard's album "Photograph" didn't really hit it big until their video depicting the murder of a movie star and a group of women locked in a cage was released.[23]

One of the largest studies (over 900 videos) classifies 46 percent as being violent. Almost half depicted violence between men and women. Some of the violence includes vignettes featuring rock stars brawling with police (Sammy Haggar in "I Can't Drive 55"), caged women (Motley Crue in "Looks That Kill"), rock idols throwing away their books and fighting with gun-toting high-school guards ("Heaven in Rock School") and a music hero electrocuting humans (Ronnie Dio in "The Last in Line").[24]

Sexually Suggestive and Occult Scenes

Violence, illicit sex and the occult seem to go hand in hand in many rock songs. The same holds true for many of today's videos. As far as the negative sexual problems, one news magazine reported that women all too often are portrayed as "bimbos." They undress in silhouette, stretch out over car hoods and snarl like animals. Their dress includes fishnet and leather.[25] Madonna, in her video "Like a Virgin," among other suggestive actions, writhes on a bed in a wedding gown. The director of the Madonna video was all cheers as he stated, "I don't see any way to be subtle with a song like that. Madonna's not subtle. She's singing about sex."[26]

The growing emphasis of occultic activity in music has

been connected directly with bizarre cases of murder and rape.

The recent rash of murders in the Los Angeles area attributed to the "Night Stalker" is one such example. In some of the homes of the victims there was found a pentagram, and other satanic symbols. At the scene of one of the murders, a baseball cap with the logo of a popular heavy-metal group accused of injecting devil worship into its music was found.[27]

The accused killer is said to have an obsession with satanic or occultic music. One of his former classmates noted that he was an avid follower of AC-DC and was particularly attracted to their 1979 hit album, "Highway to Hell."

During one of his court hearings, where he was charged with numerous counts of murder and a multitude of other felonies, the accused denied all charges and left the courtroom shouting, "Hail Satan!"[28]

A Need for Positive Christian Expression

Against this tide of visual lasciviousness, Christian artists are attempting to raise up a standard through their own religious videos. Some of these work quite well while others only offer a milder form of what the world puts out. It will take more than "Christian" girls in tight pants dancing to the lead singer's surley singing to draw the world to the Lord. Let us pray that in attempting to reach the world these artists don't copy the world so much that the message is buried in the same sensuous and abstract type of fantasy that we're trying to lead them away from.

I warmly applaud any sincere spirit-guided attempt to be creative in this area. I believe the door for positive Christian expression through this medium is wide open. The God who

31

is called Creator can certainly give us the kind of creativity that will command the attention of today's world, a world jaded by the lifeless themes of violence, sex, drugs and the occult.

TAKING INVENTORY

The following is a checklist for parents to help them in taking inventory of how much they know about what is influencing their children through the media of modern music.

	Yes	No
1. Are you aware of the kinds of music your children are listening to?	___	___
2. Do you know how much time each day your children spend listening to rock music?	___	___
3. Have you ever listened straight-through to the words of today's most popular music?	___	___
4. Can you name the rock stars or groups your children are currently listening to?	___	___
5. Have you thoroughly considered the words of some of today's "milder" pop tunes? (If so, what are the messages they are sending? Do they compare with those of rock tunes?)	___	___
6. Have you ever witnessed your children imitating in actions or clothing some of today's rock stars?	___	___
7. Are you familiar with some of the music videos on the market today?	___	___

3
Pornography
Telephone, Magazines, Films and Videos

In the '60s and early '70s, America went through what some have called a sexual revolution. Restraint was thrown out the window; casual sin was in. Yet, more recently with the advent of herpes and AIDS some have noted that there is a growing decline in promiscuous sexual relationships. The risks seem too great. A one-night stand can lead to a life-threatening disease. No doubt, this trend will continue.

Yet with this turnaround in the area of sexual activity, there is one area of perversion that is not declining; rather it is growing. Sexual fantasy will be big business in the future if what its advocates say is true. Imaginative sex is considered safe and easy. One well-known porn peddler explained in an article in *Rolling Stone* magazine this assessment of his business:

> The future is assembly line sex, not actual (sex act) . . . but fantasy.[1]

One evidence of this trend is the new market in telephone sex.

Telephone Sex

Magazine and newspaper ads advertise sex over the phone to a growing number of customers. In these ads, beautiful models express their desire to make love over the phone. Some companies even sell gift certificates. The service isn't cheap, even if it is easy to get. One phone call can be as high as $35. Yet there are millions of people out there willing to pay for it. One commentator suggested that the reason some people prefer to talk out their fantasy rather than go to a prostitute is that they actually believe they are having sex.[2]

A major San Francisco pornographer explained that as long as the caller believes he's having sex, the physical contact with the other party isn't that important. In fact, the sexual experience might even be better because the caller can picture the perfect partner, face and body. It's quite possible that those who indulge in this activity think they're not really doing anything evil or perverse, but rather just safely escaping from their humdrum life for a little mental adventure.

It's just such delusions that make the whole arena of sexual fantasy so dangerous. Unless our society determines to redeem their minds from undisciplined selfishness, the seeds of destruction being sown now will spring up into a harvest of destruction later.

History of the Modern Porno Plague

Sexual perversion and pornography have been with man for ages. I saw the evidence of this one summer while in the ancient city of Ephesus. As our guide led us through the ruins of this fascinating city where the apostle Paul witnessed such great revival, he pointed out a strange carving etched in the stone beneath our feet. There in clear sight was an advertisement for a brothel. A woman's face and a foot pointed the way to a place of sex-for-hire. Today, purveyors of illicit sex no longer chisel their promotions in stone, yet the offer still stands; sex can be purchased. And for many, pornography makes it cheap and easy.

Pornography, Not a New Issue

America was having problems with illicit material as far back as 1842, when the first federal restrictions were made against the importing of obscene pictures. Our nation's moral standards had changed radically by the middle of the twentieth century. In 1957, a district court decided that for something to be obscene it must be determined by this standard:

> Whether to the average person, applying contemporary community standards, the dominant theme of the material taken as a whole appeals to prurient interest.[3]

Later, in 1966, the definition of obscenity was restricted to include material "utterly without redeeming social value."[4] With such liberal interpretation the floodgates were opened to the pornographers.

Back in 1953 though, pornography had begun to take on new sophistication. Up until the publication of the first *Playboy* magazine, most pornography had been cheaply produced, poorly packaged and hard to get.

Playboy's first issue featured nude photos of Marilyn Monroe. *Playboy* had arrived. Its growth was phenomenal. Its first year's circulation went from 70,000 to 175,000.[5]

Twenty years later, the magazine was selling 20 million

copies a month. Soon others jumped on the bandwagon and pushed the number of pornographic magazines being published to about 400 million. It wasn't long, however, before more than nudity was being portrayed on the pages of these magazines. In the mid-'60s group sex and sex with animals found their way into print. Today, even sex with children, some as young as six months old, is being displayed in some types of perverted magazines. Two-hundred-and-fifty different types of kiddie porn magazines are being circulated in the 1980s.[6]

The same has happened in the film industry. Producers are pushing toward the outer limits of decadence. One popular perverted porno film is called *Scorcher of Hot Torcher*. It's being marketed under an ad line that reads, "super sadism at its cruelest . . . sublime agony."[7] A popular video cassette carries a similar theme. Its title is "Beat the Bitch."[8] These brief examples of porn's modern history show that this problem is not about to go away without some serious efforts on the part of concerned citizens.

Films and Video Porn

Once relegated to under-the-counter marketing, the porn industry is now breaking into every available channel used to reach the American consumer. Some of the new methods for distributing smut are potentially far more dangerous than the "dirty magazine" approach.

Modern technology can now be used to bring sexual perversion to the theaters and living rooms of America through the graphic method of live-action films and video.

For years, researchers have been aware of the typical short filmstrips that show in sex shops, but more recently X-rated films have upgraded and expanded their appeal to a more sophisticated audience. The TV news magazine *West*

57th Street reported that pornographic film producers will have made 1,700 new porn movies in 1985, while the "legitimate" Hollywood film industry will only turn out about 170 new movies.[9]

Presently there are about 700 "adult" theaters in the United States. It is estimated that the patronage at these film houses will run as high as 2 million, resulting in $500 million income for the theater owners. Producers who spend $120,000 on a typical feature-length film can expect to double their investments.[10]

What has fueled the continued growth of this type of product in theaters across America? It appears that a growing number of our countrymen are not willing to merely dream about perversion, but want an increasing detail and graphic depiction to inspire their perverted thought life.

One wonders what effect this has on marriages and relationships between sexes in our culture. It seems at a time when our culture is facing a growing struggle with lasting and solid relationships, the fantasies of film sex are working to make the true intimacy that God intended to function within marriage a potential victim. Communication and tenderness are being thrown out the door while viewers are content to get their stimulation watching others perform sexually.

With the advent of the Video Cassette Recorder (VCR), a whole new realm of potential sexual fantasy has been made available to the American public. To quote a New York pornographic magazine publisher, the potential is enormous:

> Each VCR is a potential vehicle to become a pornographic theater. This makes even the smallest town available for pornography, thus multiplying pornographic theaters a thousand-fold.[11]

Statistics seem to back up the fact that there is a growing industry in this area of sensual imagination. Nearly 70 percent of the film industry's profits are generated by the sale of video cassettes.[12] It is estimated that one-fifth of all video sales are in the category of X-rated films. A *Newsweek* magazine poll gave these shocking statistics:

> 40 percent of all VCR owners bought or rented X-rated video cassettes in 1984. A market that 5 years ago provided a porn producer with 5 percent of his profit now brings in 70 percent of his revenues.[13]

What possible effect will this present boom in the sale and rental of X-rated video cassettes have on the lives of Americans? Millions of people who would never venture into a sleazy film house can now bring the same graphic material home to view without the embarrassment of being seen in the wrong place or having to endure the company of overtly perverted individuals who frequent such places. With easy access to such grossly immoral fare, the potential for several things is evident.

First, the appetite for such perversions will only be increased and with it the desensitizing effect that porn has on the natural and biblical approach to sexuality. Second, the potential for such cassettes getting into the hands of children and minors is drastically increased. A person under the legal age is not allowed into an X-rated theater, but youngsters might easily get ahold of one of their parent's "perverted" cassettes while the adults are not at home to prevent such a tragedy. As sad as all this is, there is another area into which porn is spreading its tentacles.

Computer Sex

Today, pornographers will use any avenue available to spread their perverted ideas. One method they loudly herald as unstoppable by their religious opponents is that of modern computer technology. A new computer service known as Sextex makes it possible for its customers to communicate by their computer with X-rated stars, review ads for sexual paraphernalia and talk to other Sextex users "in an uninhibited, uncensored atmosphere for immediate gratification."[14]

Knowing the techniques that teenage computer fans have used to get into even top-secret government files, the potential for this form of porn being abused by the young is enormous. When one realizes that almost every form of communication is being tapped by perverted sex salesmen, it's enough to make you shudder at the amount of evil being carried electronically all around us (not to mention the long-standing problem of X-rated cable TV programs being pumped into American living rooms). What many parents fail to realize is that as they are becoming desensitized to perverted sex, so are their children.

A booming teenage sex film industry is causing long-standing film studios to change their productions and marketing plans. This strategy will only increase the amount of immoral propaganda American youth are having to face.

Teenage Sex Films

Increasingly, in the last 10 years film-house markees have displayed the following types of movie titles: *Hot Moves, Hard Bodies, Joysticks, My Tutor, Going All the Way, Bachelor Party, Hollywood Hot Tales, The Last American Virgin,* and *Porky's I & II*. If you haven't guessed by now, these films have one major theme underlying what are often senseless and clichéd plots: sex. The sad thing is that these films are doing an increasing business among those who least need this kind of stimulation.

One of the pioneer films in this genre, *Animal House,* was made for only $2.9 million. It went on to gross $150 million. The 1982 *Porky's* cost $4.8 million and produced $180 million in box office revenues.[15] Hollywood producers read the bottom line on this kind of film and decided to jump on the bandwagon if this is what makes money.

We need to point out that sex is not the only theme of these films, even though each film has enough salacious material to educate a growing audience of teenagers with a view of sexuality that takes it out of the pure realm God intends and places it squarely in the locker room. To the problem-plagued teenagers today, this is like pouring high-octane dragster fuel on an already out-of-control fire. Statistics tell us that today's teens are not coping well with the amount of sexual perversion being shoved their way.

One study revealed the startling effects the liberal propagation of sex is having on young people:

> Sixty percent of teens between ages 16-18 have had sexual intercourse, while 33 percent of kids between 13-15 years of age have also experienced sexual intercourse. Of those actively involved in sexual activity, almost 60 percent do not use birth-control methods, or use them only some of the time. Among teenage girls, only 13 percent would marry the father of their baby if they became pregnant, while nearly 35 percent would get abortions. Two-thirds of all teenagers would prefer to live with someone before marriage or instead of marriage.[16]

The Effects of Pornography

Perhaps the first problem with pornography is the way it fuels the fantasies of those exposed to it. One thing is certain, people fantasize often. One university study showed that most people experience seven or eight fantasies a day, and some have as many as 40 per day.[17]

But what kind of fantasies are people having? Researchers have discovered that many fantasies are perverted and some even quite frightening. Having sex with someone besides their partner was the most common fantasy among heterosexuals. Yet strangely enough, homosexual fantasies were listed fourth and fifth among heterosexuals.

As disturbing as this is, the evidence seems to point toward even more frightening activities going on in the minds of many caught up in sexual imaginations. Fantasies involving forced sexual encounters were in the top two on the list of women's fantasies and 25 percent of all fantasies that most people experience included sadomasochism, group sex and homosexuality.[18]

Although these mental images may be romantic and idealized, the preoccupation with them seems to signal a subtle acceptance of these bizarre dreams. Although some have stated that fantasies are a healthy part of a good relationship, constant fantasy can actually enlarge the gap between partners.[19]

With all this unnatural mental imagining going on, the question comes up concerning where many of these thoughts come from. Pornography has long been a recognized source for sexual fantasy. Some sexual therapists even go so far as to encourage couples to view sexually explicit material to enhance their sex lives.[20] Yet, what is the effect on communication, openness and genuine lovemaking when married

41

partners aren't thinking about one another but about some other "dream lover"?

Then there's the problem that arises from those who take their fantasies to the limit. Some even believe that those who act and pose in these strange printed sexual excesses engage in them as part of their life-style. One report has it that a former Miss America, who was dethroned for posing nude, was offended when she discovered that some held the opinion that she actually engaged in the sexual deviant activity portrayed in the *Penthouse* magazine photo of her.[21]

Many who are caught up in fantasies actually prefer them to reality. It's easier to control and mold unreal images and daydreams. But when these daydreams begin to spill over into reality the problems tend to multiply. Studies have shown that pornography leads to sexual deviance even in normal people.

An organization known as the Free Congress Foundation detailed that porn is used by the majority of violent sex offenders.[22] With rapes having increased by more than 700 percent since 1933, no wonder psychologists are finding the link between violent sexual crimes and pornography a conclusion reinforced by their studies.[23]

Research has concluded that even brief exposure to filmed scenes of rape can propel the viewer toward antisocial behavior. It can also reinforce the concept that women want to be raped.[24] Individuals watching this type of fantasy may not respond to real violence in a normal fashion.[25]

The FBI, in a special study, interviewed 36 convicted sex killers. From their research they discovered some startling facts: The killers have had long-standing fantasies that were just as real to them as the acts themselves; the killers' biggest sexual focus was reading sexually explicit materials; the majority of the perpetrators eventually attempted to act out their fantasies on their victims. The tendency to get bored at a certain level and then go on to the more bizarre was also the case, stated one of the killers.[26]

It can be argued that the large majority of pornography readers will not be violent sex offenders. Yet pornography's power most certainly will have some kind of negative effect on a normal, healthy individual. With foreign issues of *Playboy* introducing girls as young as 16 to its pages, those who view such displays of adolescent nudity will be tempted more than ever to accept sex with minors as normal behavior in our society.[27]

Researcher Judith Reisman showed that *Penthouse, Playboy* and *Hustler* magazines contain cartoons depicting children having sex with older people.[28] Gradually, our society is being pushed to the limits of perversion. Magazines like those mentioned can be found in convenience stores and often are within easy reach of minors.

With famous TV stars and a former politician's wife posing for nude photo sessions, Americans have been asked to accept such behavior as a sophisticated and normal part of our culture. Women who display themselves for such pictures are not only hurting themselves, but also those who love them. In an interview with the boyfriend of a *Playboy* centerfold, he told of the rage he felt toward the photographers who took the pictures, as well as his embarrassment knowing his friends, along with millions of other American men, would be lustfully beholding her naked body.[29]

Pornographers are pushing the outer limits of perversion. Women bound and chained being whipped for the pleasure of the viewer can be seen in special peep shows across the country. Other films show a man who pays a prostitute to call him dogface and beat him until he puts on a dog chain, barks like a dog and eats from a dog dish.[30]

One thing is clear, whether it be hard-core or soft-core, pornography is having its effect on our society. If fantasies can be bought for the right price, then perhaps soon the realities that Americans have considered normal for decades will be pushed aside to be replaced by displays of perversion to feed the appetites of those who have the money to pay for these wares of decadence. Fantasies like these should never become reality, yet the evidence shows that sadly this is not the case.

TAKING INVENTORY

1. Many reports indicate a link between pornography and violent sex crimes, yet there are still those who argue that there is no connection whatsoever. How do you and your family members feel about this controversy? What can you use to support your answers?

2. Our author reminds us that sex is God's idea and within the context of marriage it is a beautiful experience. However, sex outside of marriage (fornication) is sin. With your family, search the Scriptures for what God has to say about this all-important issue. For starters, see 1 Corinthians 7:2 and 1 Thessalonians 4:3. What others can you find?

4
Role-Playing and the Occult

Games, Cartoons, Toys and Comics

America is in the midst of an occult revival. Researchers claim there are some 600,000 practitioners of this ancient art in the United States today.[1] About 10,000 astrologers extend their services to the public, some charging as much as $300 for their advice.[2] Over 100 psychic fairs are held in shopping malls across this country every year. The 300 psychics staffing them charge $10 for a 15-minute session.

As shocking as all this is, perhaps an even greater danger is in the glamorizing of witchcraft that is being presented to young people through fantasy role-playing games. If America is reeling under the present wave of occultic interest, what will happen with the generation that's now growing up with wizards and witches as heroes?

Board games have long been an enjoyable pastime for Americans. Who hasn't spent an evening with family or friends rolling dice across the table and moving a game piece up some imaginary street buying property and hoping to become a big-time tycoon. Yet compared to the present phenomena of fantasy games the old-fashioned games of 30 or 40 years ago seem mild.

Today's games have become total-involvement experiences. The game *Photon*, mentioned earlier in this book, is a good example. Those who regularly participate in this space-age entertainment may find it's more than a mild distraction, as a *Newsweek* article on the subject suggested:

> The biggest risk in Photon may be its addictive nature; some devotees manage to spend as much as $100 a day.[3]

Perhaps the reason for the strong appeal games have is their ability to help us escape for a while from the pressures of daily living. One mother who regularly brings her kids and relatives to play *Photon* says, "You just get out of your life for a while. It's an escape sort of thing."[4]

The future possibilities of escape fantasy seem unlimited as modern technology links up with the human imagination. Interactive laser-disc games are one example of this. Some of these are murder mysteries with multiple endings, allowing the players to select several possible answers to imaginary crimes, as they listen and watch for clues. There's even a feature that lets you interview a possible suspect in the make-believe drama.[5]

As to the future popularity of such games, only time will tell. But from the looks of things, some computer scientists see the development of "hardware and software" that will completely involve the game enthusiast in his make-believe world. Large computer-controlled screens, sonar systems to detect body movement, an interactive playsuit and sensory feedback equipment would be used to allow players to swing imaginary swords and have an on-screen figure do the same.[6] If it all sounds rather sophisticated and expensive, don't forget that when the first computer chips were produced their price was prohibitive to the common consumer. Today they can be purchased for just a few dollars.

Yet, if it's total involvement the player wants, he need go no further than his college campus to find some students playing games like *Assassin*. Using toy weapons, players put out "contracts" on other students and if they find their opponents alone and unprotected they will "terminate" them.

One such evening of game-playing left a student at California State University Long Beach with a near-fatal wound from a campus policeman's real gun. The student was shot when he pointed his simulated M-16 weapon at the officer. One campus official expressed his concern to the media: "What was considered fun and games for the students almost caused at least one death."[7]

Another fad which has sprouted up in recent years has made a business out of these types of escapes. The *National Survival Game* is reported to have had more than 345,000 players in 1985.[8] The participants in this "shoot-em-up" fantasy dress like military SWAT teams and go after each other, shooting paint pellets that "eliminate" other players when struck. The devotees claim it's all great fun especially when they capture their opponent's flag. Players have developed names for their teams like: Faces of Death Ha-Ha, Land Sharks, Devils, Painters and 12-Man Jury. Between 8,000-10,000 people play the Survival Game each weekend.[9]

Looking at all of this enthusiasm for games of death and danger, one could easily relegate it all to the harmless release of energy in a society where men and women spend too much time behind desks in stuffy office buildings and are just looking for a release. Without a doubt, many will successfully argue that point. But perhaps the real scare in all of this present fascination with gaming is the possible effect it has on young, impressionable minds.

In Newton, Massachusetts, a teacher was shocked to discover some fifth and sixth graders playing a game that she felt was taking the whole thing just a little too far. The youngsters were playing at being big-time drug dealers. They used flour for cocaine, oregano for marijuana and Monopoly money for cash. When the instructor found out about it she had a long talk with the students and told them to quit playing the game.[10]

Most people would be in agreement with the teacher's actions, realizing that what often starts out as play has the potential of becoming a permanent part of one's life-style. It's with this kind of heartfelt concern that the subject of occult fantasy games are discussed in the following segment.

Occult Fantasy Games

Of the estimated one dozen fantasy role-playing games on the market, the most popular is Dungeons and Dragons®. The following scenario, quoted from an article by the Jesus People U.S.A. Productions, gives a picture of the game playing that goes on in this imaginary world:

> Our company has entered into the dark cavernous labyrinthine corridor, weapons drawn, frightened at facing the imminent danger they know will be awaiting them with each approaching step toward the fiery monster's lair.
>
> "Should I go first?" questions our five-foot companion, his elfish features contorting with anticipated agitation.
>
> "No," whispers the druid. "Perhaps I can

charm this giant reptilian creature with a potion that will not allow him to achieve consciousness."

The camera focuses and we see five humans hunched over a dining room table. Four are emphatically arguing out the best way to deal with the danger while one, seated behind propped up school folders to hide his array of maps and graphs, smugly looks on. He is in no danger. In fact, the medieval setting and reptilian creature are of his imagination. He, as DM, or Dungeon Master, is the creator, narrator and referee of this fantasy world.

Player I: (hobbit) "Let's split."

Player IV: (druid) "No way! There's treasures in there for sure."

Player I: "What good's treasure if we're dead?"

DM: "The creature is awakening. He senses your presence in the corridor."

Player III: (cleric) "I contact my 'familiar' stationed at the outside entrance. Is the flying dragon in sight?"

DM: (rolling one of the many odd-shaped dice in front of him to check out the odds of the dragon being there) "He sees nothing."

Player I: "I'm turning invisible."

Player IV: "Chicken."

DM: "He's nearing the entrance to the hall."

Player II: (elf) "I draw my magic bow with the black arrow."

Player I: "I'm running down the hall about 50 yards."

Player III: (rummaging frantically through a pile of books on the table) "I found it! I throw a sleeping spell toward the creature."

DM: "No good. He wasn't into the hall yet. Your spell went harmlessly by. But the reptile sensed the magic passing and stepping back is roaring in rage."

All Players: (groan)

Player III: "And it was my last spell for this day."

DM: "He rushes into the halls. Fumes and fire spewing from his nostrils."

Player II: "I unleash my arrow."

DM: (rolling a dice again, checking the odds of contact on a sliding scale in front of him) "You hit!" (rolling again) "It went in through the left eye. He's in a blinding fury now. You have four seconds before he's upon you."

Player III: "If I grab the others' hands and teleport, will they go with me?"

DM: "You'll have to try to know."

Player III: "Quick, give me your hands. I teleport outside the caverns."

DM: (rolling dice) "It worked. You're all outside except the hobbit who you couldn't possibly have touched 50 yards away."

Player I: "I'm running as fast as I can. Guys, help me!"

Player IV: "Serves you right. You weren't going to help us."

DM: "The creature checks himself in mid-flight in confusion as he passes the spot where you stood. But he smells and hears the hobbit farther ahead and charges on."

Player I: "Help me."

Player IV: "Fat chance."

Player III: "I teleport back to the hobbit."

DM: (rolling dice) "You're there."

Player III: "I grab him and teleport back to the entrance."

DM: (rolling dice again) "No good. There's enough power left for only one of you. Leave him. Or you both stay. You have four seconds."

Player I: "Don't leave me. I have no powers."

Player III: "What's the use of us both dying . . . I'm going."

DM: "You're gone. You have two seconds left."

Player I: (helplessly) "I turn and throw my dagger."

DM: (rolling dice) "Totally useless. It's like throwing a pin at an elephant. He doesn't even bother to eat you because you're a burnt little crisp from the fire as he rushes onward toward the entrance."

Player I: "Ugh! I'm dead. I can't believe it."[11]

To the typical 12- or 13-year-old player, such action and adventure sounds like an exciting way to spend an evening. But there are enough warning signs and questions surrounding this phenomenon to give some serious thought to its potential dangers.

Occultic Connections

Of first concern is the game's link to the occult. D & D® instruction manuals, with names like Players Handbook,

Dungeon Masters Guide, Deities and Demigods, give details about the use of spells and magic. Certain players may take on the role of a "cleric," one with the power to resist the undead, demons and devils.[12] Spell casters in the game use magic circles, pentagrams and occultic triangles.[13]

Experts in the occult know these symbols are commonly used in witchcraft and Satan worship. Serving a deity or demigod is also a significant part of the game.[14] Many of these supernatural beings are well-known heathen gods, some being specifically named in the Bible as abominations. An example would be the Canaanite god, Molech, who is on the cover of one of these manuals. Some of the ancient Jews, who had turned away from Jehovah, offered their children as burnt sacrifices to these pagan deities. To play this game the participant may choose to align himself with just such a demonic force.

One avid player commented that in D & D® it was more advantageous to be evil. If you're an evil character, there is no penalty for chopping down someone from behind.[15] One investigator into the dangers of the game gave his comments about its possible power to indoctrinate someone into evil demonic religion. Dr. Gary North wrote his concerns in a Dec. 5, 1980, edition of *Remnant Review,* published in Phoenix, Arizona:

> Without any doubt in my own mind, after years of study of the history of occultism, after having researched a book on the topic, and after having consulted with scholars in the field of historical research, I can say with confidence: These games are the most effective, most magnificently packaged, most profitably marketed, most thoroughly researched introduction to the occult in man's

recorded history . . . . This is no game.

In the Scriptures God has given clear warning about involvement with the forces of sorcery. Even if the D & D® advocate claims that they're only playing at such fantasies, he should realize that these types of games are based on real principles of witchcraft and magic, and that those who practice witchcraft suffer the danger of being under God's retribution. Deuteronomy 18:9-14 says:

> When you come into the land which the LORD your God is giving you, you shall not learn to follow the abominations of those nations. There shall not be found among you *anyone* who makes his son or daughter pass through the fire, *or one* who practices witchcraft, *or* a soothsayer, or one who interprets omens, or a sorcerer, or one who conjures spells, or a medium, or a spiritist, or one who calls up the dead. For all who do these things *are* an abomination to the LORD, and because of these abominations the LORD your God drives them out from before you. You shall be blameless before the LORD your God. For these nations which you will dispossess listened to soothsayers and diviners; but as for you, the LORD your God has not appointed such for you *(NKJV)*.

Also, Deuteronomy 7:26 reads:

> Nor shall you bring an abomination into your house, lest you be doomed to destruction like it; *but* you shall utterly detest it and utterly abhor it, for it *is* an accursed thing *(NKJV)*.

Violence

Another concern surrounding fantasy role-playing games is the tendency towards vivid portrayal of gruesome violence and perverted sexuality.

John Eric Holms, a brain scientist who has been a practicing Dungeon Master, wrote in an article on D & D® this startling observation:

> The level of violence in this make-believe world runs high. There's hardly a game in which the players do not indulge in murder, arson, torture, rape or highway robbery.[16]

In his quest, the player has the option of hiring creatures who can be expected to rape and loot and even eat their captives.[17] The player is also instructed how best to perform the assassination of a target character.[18] In the Deities and Demigods Manual, the Rain God Tlaloc festival is described. Numbers of babies are sacrificed to this deity after which the priests cook and eat them.[19] It's hard to imagine that a player could possibly be encouraged to align himself with such a being, make-believe or not.

There should be little doubt left in the mind of anyone taking the time to study the detailed instructions for this game that excessive and brutal violence is almost gleefully expounded as a factor in the alluring excitement of this game. For parents of children and teenagers exposed to D & D®, one wonders if they might have second thoughts about allowing them to play the game.

Perverted Sexuality

New West magazine, in its report on the D & D® phenomenon, mentioned the fantasy role-playing game *Arduin*

Grimori. Its creator's ideas were shocking. The game's "critical hit table" is a detailed example of sadistic pornography.[20] Other commentators have explained how creatures and players in the game are involved in seduction and sexual assault.[21] There are also detailed descriptions on the types of sexual perverts and venereal diseases one might encounter while playing the game.[22]

Role-Playing

The fact that these games are called role-playing games adds another factor to our concern over their dangers. The D & D® inventor explained, "You have to pursue D & D with your entire soul if you're going to do well at it."[23] A player pursuing this game with all his heart and then taking on the identity of certain characters in the play action might be risking more than an evening of wasted time, as some suggest in their lawsuit against such companies as the producers of D & D®.[24] Claims have been made that those involved in the game have committed suicide after having a spell cast on them. And the list of those who have suffered deep depression after playing D & D® continues to grow.

Separating reality from fantasy becomes increasingly difficult as one involves himself fully in the game. One player stated that he was so much into the game that the majority of the time he actually became the person he fantasized to be:

> I am Dungeon Master 98 percent of the time. I am the god of my world, the creator who manipulates the gods and humans. But my bossiness has extended itself into real life. I've exploited and abused people. People have hated me for it . . . . It's hazardous! Your vocabulary, your mental

quickness increases, but school seems increasingly boring and droll. Your grades drop. The more time you spend in your fantasy world, the more you want to walk away from this world. The whole thing is getting very bad.[25]

The nature of D & D® is such that a player can be consumed with the game throughout the course of the day. Whether he is studying, waiting for a bus or driving a car, the player's mind can be wrapped up in strategy and planning, as described in the following article:

When not actually playing, Gary spends his evenings on dungeon diagrams, character records and descriptions of new monsters, deities and spells, which so far have filled 1,500 pages. In class, he daydreams about the traps and tortures that will await his friends as soon as he can shuck the humdrum guise of high school junior and, in a blinding metamorphosis, become a wizard, a god.[26]

Why is there such power over the mind in D & D®? Could it be its close connection with occultic practice? Obviously, it is not packaged as a "satanic" board game for young and old alike. But the premise it operates on is clearly from the demonic realm.

The fact that this game, which glamorizes witchcraft, has become so popular is just one more sign of a growing trend among Americans toward the occult. Isaiah 59:19 tells us that the enemy shall come in like a flood. Revelation 12:13-15 speaks of the dragon sending out a flood after the woman and the man child. Certainly Satan's plan is to destroy the innocent and godly with a flood of evil. In many ways, sorcerers appear to be replacing true prophets of God. The Bible lists some of these false teachers and warns about involvement with them. They can be identified by the following names:

> Magicians, astrologers, chaldeans, soothsayers, wisemen, magi, sorcerers, wizards, diviners, observers of times, enchanters, witches, consulters with familiar spirits and necromancers (see Deut. 18).

Those who are involved in such practices may find themselves in league with the sorcerers of old. When the apostle Paul confronted one of the false prophets of his day on the Isle of Cyprus, he had many negative comments concerning the corrupt character of Elymas, the magician: Elymas was full of subtlety and mischief, a child of the devil, the enemy of righteousness, a perverter of the right way of the Lord (see Acts 13:8-10).

Modern-day sorcerers promise much. They claim to tell the future, talk to lost loved ones, give you power over others and even· curse your enemies. All of this for a fee, of course. The ancient false prophet Baalam was engaged to curse Israel (see Num. 22:7). He too was a psychic for hire.

These occultists have enchantments but they are no match for the finger of God (see Exod. 8:19). They are unable to stand against God's true prophets (see Exod. 9:11). The Bible tells us that ultimately those who propagate and practice such things will be brought down:

> Just as Jannes and Jambres opposed Moses, so also these men oppose the truth—men of

depraved minds, who, as far as the faith is concerned, are rejected. But they will not get very far because, as in the case of those men, their folly will be clear to everyone (2 Tim. 3:8,9, *NIV*).

And for those who might fear the power of some spell or curse, God's Word promises protection for those who follow Him and do not dabble in the occult:

There is no sorcery against Jacob, no divination against Israel (Num. 23:23, *NIV*).

With such powerful directives given in the Scriptures, it is no wonder that many spiritual leaders are warning people about the dangers of D & D® and many other fantasy role-playing games. Skeptics can always argue that to them it's only a game, just a harmless pastime. But why would someone want to even toy around with something God says is a deceptive and destructive force?

Fads come and go and perhaps fantasy role-playing games will go the way of other crazes, but what will happen to those who have opened themselves up to such detailed instruction in a game that many Christian leaders clearly believe to be a primer in the occultic arts?

Occultic Cartoons, Toys and Comics
While covering so many aspects of fantasy in our culture, it would be an oversight not to touch upon the area of cartoons, toys and comic books.

In a society that is becoming increasingly illiterate, America's appetite for the less complicated forms of entertainment is increasing. TV cartoons are often substituted for good books. The Saturday morning children's TV "ghetto" has become not only a sensory entertainment orgy, but also a source of indoctrination. Children are being taught the occult through these shows. Comic books are becoming one of the major reading materials for millions of teenagers and young adults. Animated features and toy spin-offs, along with comic books, are a potential destructive force that parents would do well to investigate.

Occultic Cartoons

In the last 20 years we've come a long way from the wholesome cartoon age of innocency. As commentator Winkie Pratney pointed out in an interview for a documentary on fantasy, the distinction between adult and child has broken down. Adult themes are often introduced to children without a second thought as to the possible effect these ideas can have on young impressionable minds. Phil Phillips, who has written an excellent tract on the subject of imagination and children, stresses that childhood is the time when our imaginations are being developed, and Satan's plan is clearly to interject as much of his vain imaginations into our thought lives as possible. With children watching 15,000-22,000 hours of TV before they graduate from high school, the possible absorption of false teaching through this medium is immense.[27]

One of the leading cartoon series on TV today is *Masters of the Universe,* which features occult images and magical forces. The hero and heroine in this series gain their strength from a spiritual force that can be used by good and evil agents alike.[28] Analogies can be seen between the heroine and ancient Egyptian paganism.[29]

Joining these super heroes in the cartoon world are other features like *Dungeons and Dragons®, Blackstar* and *Thundercats,* all of which have a strong dose of magic and occultism thrown in. Cartoon witchcraft is not limited merely to the more aggressive style of animated feature. Even the more gentle and sweet appearing programs can have subtle but strong reference to the demonic. An example would be the Smurf show. While looking innocent and cute at first glance, closer examination shows its characters trusting in spells and incantations for deliverance.[30]

Often parents are tempted to simply let their children watch cartoons trusting that the networks and station programmers will have the children's best interest in mind. But strong concerns from such groups as ACT (Action for Children's Television) suggest that the bottom line often may be profits.[31] Promoted by the "He-Man" series, Mattel Toys has sold more than 70 million plastic "tie-in" toys in a three-year period.[32] It is now possible for children to not only watch these characters, but to play with them as well.

Toys That Teach Witchcraft

These "animated sales catalogs," as one commentator describes TV cartoon shows with toy spin-offs,[33] may also be helping to promote sorcery among the younger generation. There's a general consensus among child psychologists that the kinds of toys children play with can influence their psychological growth. In that regard, toys and playthings that focus the child's attention on the demonic could also instill evil values. Children growing up in Nazi Germany were encouraged to play with toy-sized torture devices. They were taught how to use them in the hopes of instilling specific values in the lives of these children.[34]

Although playing with occultic toys doesn't always guarantee the child will grow up desiring to live out these fantasies, we cannot dismiss the possibility that they may. A parent should not sluff off this concern without asking some serious questions about the possible dangers out there.

The apostle Paul warns that in the last days many will be seduced by doctrines of devils and satanic wonders (see 1 Tim. 4:1; 2 Thess. 2:9,10). Perhaps those who will be so deceived will at least have been partially programmed for it through an ever-increasing diet of occultic cartoons and toys.

Other toys that stray into this area of sorcery are Power Lords, Dungeons and Dragons®, Star Wars and Crystlar Figures. There are others which are not mentioned here and discerning parents need to study and be aware of the types of playthings and programs being offered to their children.

Comics and Confusion

Almost hand in hand with cartoons and toys is the growing comic book fad that is reinforcing young people's interest in false spiritual values.

The comic book came of age in the 1930s, at a time when many were seeking an escape from the woes and worries of the depression era. This came to be known as the golden era in comic book history.[35] Since that time, a new age known as the "silver age" has seen the genre mature into a huge industry that reaches not only children and teens but a large group in their 20s. The more adult form of this phenomenon is populated by a group that spends as much as $50 a month to read the latest episodes in the lives of their imaginary heroes. It's estimated that there are close to 3,000 specialty outlets, the majority found in shopping malls, that dispense a wide array of these comics.[36]

At first glance this whole issue could be ignored as a passing fad that is merely allowing some bored youths to waste a Saturday wandering in a cerebral amusement park. But the subculture that's grown up around this industry appears to have a more serious opinion of the messages coming through in these stories.

Some of the creators of these fantasy magazines see themselves as teachers and molders of their readers' imaginations. Frank Miller, one of the top writers in the industry, expressed his convictions to one interviewer when he said, "I don't believe it's the responsibility of the artist to spoonfeed the audience what they want, because the artist is bringing something to the audience, and just as the artist can learn from his audience, the audience can learn from the artist."[37]

Many comic book stories will have mini-sermons interjected between the action.[38] These dramatic lectures are no doubt filled with the creator's particular philosophy or religious viewpoint, as is clear from the comic E-Man who mockingly attacks evangelical Christianity and its struggle against secular humanism.[39]

Often the heroes who live in the pages of these stories are teams of godlike people whose membership includes individuals with occultic powers. Their names seem to confirm this: The New Teen Titans and The Uncanny X-Men. The X-Men's captain is Storm, a witch who can manipulate nature's forces, such as the wind.[40]

Sex is another subject that is not left untouched in many of these issues. And although only one segment of the comic industry includes pornographic comics, many of these editions show the heroes and heroines in the sack together.

Perhaps the final negative element in many of the comics that are part of this current phenomenon is their pervading sense of gloom. Many of them have themes that show that the future belongs to the oppressors.[41] A sense of hopelessness and cynicism dominates the lives of many of the characters.

Parents who have children reading these types of comics

should beware. Needless to say, adults who are feeding on these stories should take to heart the warning expressed earlier.

There is a fearful possibility that such activities are preparing some of our youth of today to become modern pagans. Another generation is arising that has been spoonfed on the occult and witchcraft. We must seriously consider the possibility that they will grow up and replace solid biblical faith of past generations with a religion rebirthed from the Dark Ages.

TAKING INVENTORY

1. Are you or any of your family members players of some sort of the role-playing games addressed in this chapter? If so, have you ever had the feeling there was sorcery involved? Have you ever questioned the various rules and regulations of the games? Explain your answers.

2. Are you familiar with the list of false teachers whom we are told to avoid as named in Deuteronomy 18? To review, they are: magicians, astrologers, chaldeans, soothsayers, wisemen, magi, sorcerers, wizards, diviners, observers of times, enchanters, witches, consulters with familiar spirits and necromancers. Relate these names to those in the world today with whom Christians should have no dealings.

3. In comparing toys and comics with those of years ago, what are today's playthings seeming to say to our young people? In other words, what kinds of influences are these playthings having on our youth?

5
Films

Fantasy and Science Fiction

Perhaps one of the most subtle areas of fantasy's deception is the present wave of science fiction films. These movies are some of the most entertaining dramas to come along in years. Young people, as well as adults, have slapped down their hard-earned dollars to see such visual extravaganzas as *StarWars, Close Encounters of the Third Kind* and *E.T., The Extraterrestrial.* These films have been blockbusters. They have made fortunes for their producers and directors. They may also have changed the way a whole generation will view religion.

Possibly one of the major factors in the paganizing of the younger generation has been the philosophies these films have introduced. Although it's doubtful there's any conscious human conspiracy behind this new thrust, it does seem interesting that over and over again the mystical and supernatural comes into play in each of these stories. Finding fault with E.T. and Yoda appears to be legalistic nitpicking to some, but as we examine the ideas put forth in

Star Wars, Close Encounters and *E.T.,* a different opinion may become apparent.

Star Wars

The granddaddy of the present phenomenon of science fiction and fantasy films is the trilogy known as the *Star Wars* Saga. In *Star Wars, The Empire Strikes Back* and *The Return of the Jedi* the viewer is introduced to lasers and light speed, warriors and wizards, droids and dungeons, a pirate and a princess, all smoothly delivered up in a fast-paced, action-filled adventure so enthralling that it seems to end too quickly. *Star Wars* alone has grossed over $530 million worldwide.[1]

The popularity of this film series speaks well of its director/producer, George Lucas. This young, creative genius must be credited for his talent and labor in putting together such a fascinating production. Yet it's important to examine some of the religious philosophy he's injected into his epics.

The Force

Lucas claims he got his idea for "the Force" from the writings of Carlos Casteneda, a popular author among college students.[2] One of the main characters in Casteneda's books is a Yaqui Indian sorcerer who introduces him to the occult and magical world of an alternate reality. Although these writings had a wide following on college campuses, it took a movie like *Star Wars* to popularize them and expose their concepts of "magical forces" to a younger audience.

Often sincerely religious people have found much that speaks of good in Lucas's concepts. But a closer examination of his ideas bears looking at. If the Force truly is a good concept then how is it possible that men can use this same

65

force for evil (i e , Darth Vader using the dark side of the force) It appears that this dual-sided energy field lies more in the realm of Taoism This ancient, eastern religion says both good and evil must exist together for there to be a balance in the universe

It's possible that Lucas was only looking for a unique and updated version of the traditional good-guy-versus-bad-guy scenario. But perhaps there was a clear understanding and plan behind the occult message of his epic. His comments to the news media have shown his personal views about the psychic. He gave the following definition of the Force to a *Newsweek* reporter in an article about *The Empire Strikes Back*.

> If you use it well you can see the future and past, you can sort of read minds, and you can levitate and use the whole netherworld of psychic energy.[3]

To the *Star Wars'* creator this idea may merely be a useful vehicle to help build his plot, but perhaps what he hasn't realized is the possible impact the glorifying of such magical powers has in the mind of the young viewer. The *Star Wars* trilogy clearly romanticizes several dangerous occultic phenomena.

Obi Wan Kanobi's reoccurring voice and visage fall into the category of necromancy, the practice of interaction with apparitions from beyond the grave. The Bible clearly warns such practices are denounced by God (see Deut. 18:9-11).

Levitation used by Luke Skywalker's mystical instructor is a common display of demonic powers in pagan cultures. Yoda, the little muppet who becomes Luke Skywalker's teacher, was purposely portrayed as a mystical guru, as is clear from the words of Irvin Kershner, the director of *The Empire Strikes Back*

> I wanna introduce some Zen here because I don't want the kids to walk away just feeling that everything is shoot 'em up, but that there's also a little something to think about here in terms of yourself and your surroundings.[4]

Thinking about yourself and your surroundings is a good thing, but when a little muppet who becomes a hero in the viewers' eyes lays out a line of Buddhism, one wonders just what exactly Hershner wants our young audience to think about. One of the actors in *The Empire Strikes Back* was Billy Dee Williams, who told a *Rolling Stone* magazine writer that he has been involved in Zen for 14 years. In Williams's opinion, Yoda was a type of Zen master.[5]

In the January 22, 1986, edition of the *Wall Street Journal* Lucas explained *Star Wars* as his attempt "to come up with a perspective on God." Certainly this statement seems to confirm the intended spiritual message of these films.

All of this concern could be laughed off as being overly protective, if it weren't for the fact that the film heroes do more than merely entertain. Often they mold the younger viewers' picture of reality. And when that view of reality has such a pagan slant to it, we need to ask what the eventual outcome will be.

C.S. Lewis, in his famous *The Screwtape Letters*, outlines the dangers of accepting a concept such as the Force. The following is an excerpt from that book as an elder devil is giving advice to his younger charge:

> I have great hopes that we shall learn, in due

67

time, how to emotionalize and mythologize their science to such an extent that what is, in effect, a belief in us (though not under that name) will creep in while the human mind remains closed to belief in the Enemy (God). The "Life Force," the worship of sex, and some aspects of Psychoanalysis may here prove useful. If once we can produce our perfect work—the Materialist Magician, the man, not using, but veritably worshipping, what he vaguely called "Forces" while denying the existence of "spirits"—then the end of the war will be in sight.[6]

With the success of films like *Star Wars* we can see that Lewis's insights are even more relevant today than when he wrote them several years ago.

Close Encounters of the Third Kind

This awe-inspiring cinematic masterpiece has left more theatergoers with a religious experience than perhaps any film to date. *Time* magazine, in its review of the film, gave this insightful evaluation:

In Spielberg's benign view, the confrontation between human and alien is an ecstatic evolutionary adventure, rather than a lethal star war, it is a wondrous opportunity for man to be reborn.[7]

Reborn indeed, and into what? Rebirth is certainly a well-worn religious phrase, but aptly chosen to describe the overall effect of the alien visitors on many of the humans portrayed in the film. The concept of evolution being aided by aliens is one that reoccurs in various science-fiction novels and films.

68

Who are these benign-appearing creatures that have come to guide mankind upward in his quest for life? Is there any chance that these film creatures could be forerunners of future counterparts that will do more than step out of a spaceship? What are the guidelines for good and bad aliens? Who's to say what's alien? A spaceman or a demon disguised as an interplanetary advisor sent to this dimension to open up man's understanding of the cosmic realms?

Newsweek magazine, January 1, 1979, had the following comment on the religious aspects of science-fiction films:

> People can croak "Entertainment, Entertainment!" until they're blue in the face. The fact remains that films like *Close Encounters of the Third Kind, Superman,* or even *Star Wars* have become jerry-built substitutes for the great myths and rituals of belief, hope and redemption that cultures used to shape before mass secular society took over.

To say that such films do not have an impact on what people believe would be to deny the fact that over 23 distinct denominations have resulted from purported contact with flying-saucer beings.[8]

Irving Hexham, in an article for *His* magazine, confirms this opinion. He states that films like *Close Encounters* tend to popularize esoteric beliefs. Popular books and magazines publish the experiences of people who have encountered spiritual forces and cosmic beings:

> With the help of the media, these myths enter the lives of ordinary people, who in turn begin to look and long for these experiences in order to

confirm their awakened beliefs. Once these beliefs take hold of a person's mind, they make him or her easy prey for thousands of "spiritual" groups offering to give them direction and fellowship to deepen and sustain these beliefs. TM, Hare Krishna, the Unification Church and a host of other sects share the bedrock of the new mythology and its direct assault upon the Christian faith.[9]

Something even more interesting as far as *Close Encounters* is concerned is the involvement of a member of the scientific community in its production. Noted astronomer Allen Hynek was technical advisor on the film and even had a brief cameo appearance in the movie. Such endorsements give an increasing legitimacy to the flying-saucer phenomenon.

This author personally talked with Dr. Hynek after he lectured at California State University in Chico. During the lecture, attended by over 1,000 people, the noted scientist made a brief allusion to the possibility that UFOs were not from other planets but actually from another dimension. In fact, he made the following comments to an interviewer for the *Sacramento Bee* sometime later:

> Maybe these are metaterrestrial vs. extraterrestrial [meaning UFOs are very close, rather than from outer space]. Like a parallel reality, another dimension, and it's a breaking through from one reality to another (ours).
>
> It would be like a blind person suddenly achieving sight for a few seconds and being able to glimpse the world around him—a different reality from his normal state of life.[10]

When I spoke with Dr. Hynek backstage, I asked him if he had been referring to a possible spiritual reality when he mentioned that these beings could be from another dimension. He responded by saying that in his opinion, "this is what the religious and mystical people had been saying for ages." After leaving the lecture, I reflected later how interesting it was that we now have a scientist who has adopted a belief in the supernatural under the guise of scientific research.

But what guidelines can modern investigators use when they have rejected the Bible, which is the final authority on such matters? How will the investigators know, should they ever have a close encounter with such trans-dimensional creatures, if they are divine or demonic?

E.T., The Extraterrestrial

This brilliantly produced film was designed to make the audience fall in love with its "cute" and angelic hero. A reviewer for the *Toronto Star,* under the heading, "Have a Really Happy Cry," gave the following observation of E.T.'s impact:

> I expected the four-year old in front of us to commence fidgetting the moment the opening credits were over; instead, she (he?) sat gape-mouthed for two hours, her impressionable mind clearly compelled by the unfolding story. She, like most youngsters, will accept E.T. on its most immediate level.[11]

Accepting *E.T.* on its most immediate level has major repercussions when you consider the message that comes through in this very heartwarming, but deceptive film. The largest-grossing film in history ($619 million at the time of this writing),[12] *E.T.* has presented us with a counterfeit Christ.

I can almost hear the rumble of outrage right now. "How could anyone accuse this beautiful story of being inspired by the devil? Its loving message has touched so many children."

Well, first of all, let's look at what's really coming through in all of this. Consider E.T.'s powers. Like Jesus, he healed, communicated without a spoken language, levitated or ascended, just to name a few. There's even a death and resurrection sequence. All of these virtues clearly have Christlike connotations.

In fact, Albert E. Miller, Jr., a chairman of the English department at Christopher Newport College in Newport News, Virginia, was so impressed with the parallels between E.T. and Jesus that he put together a small booklet entitled, "E.T., You're More Than a Star." In the booklet, now forced out of print by a lawsuit from Universal Studios, Miller listed 33 different characteristics he believes are similar to those of Jesus.[13] Yet in all the display of these powers, there is never any suggestion they come from God. In fact, these powers tend to glorify E.T. rather than God.

One could easily go away from the film with the idea that these types of abilities are OK when in fact the Scriptures point out that the display and use of such miraculous virtues, without God's name and clear endorsement on them, leaves one to conclude that they must come from a source outside of God's Kingdom. All such "gifts" fall into the realm the Bible calls sorcery.

Most Americans are not about to swallow the old witch on her broom idea as plausible or even desirable. Yet, when you have a gentle and loving creature from a civilization whose technology is advanced far beyond that of earth, and he's doing "wonders" like thought control and floating bicycles through the sky, it not only appears exciting, but possible.

The idea of magic being a higher level of technology keeps popping up over and over again in the films and fiction of the space age. If magic is just a higher form of technology then why not jump on the cosmic bandwagon and use this new source of power. The only problem is that when you get to the core of all these scenarios, the occultic and demonic show up. The same Spielberg who gave us *Close Encounters of the Third Kind* and *E.T.* will produce a film like *Poltergeist*, where the "spirits" are displaying the same types of "talents" that the beautiful characters from space do in his other films.

Taking these powers out of the forbidden realm of myth and making them appear to be universal has made the occult attractive, while at the same time has made the God of the Bible seem "out of it." Parents need to ask themselves if they're prepared to answer the kind of questions a child or young person will have after watching these types of films or if they're prepared to handle the problems that come if the kids don't ask but rather accept the message that the occult is exciting and perhaps even available to them. The aim of *E.T.* is quite apparent; it's a children's film, for the child in all of us. But assuming that the 5-, 10-, or 15-year-old will have the ability to discern the fantasies from the reality is another thing altogether.

The whole idea of the younger generation being the primary target of a new wave of occultic influence is the theme of a science-fiction novel by Arthur C. Clarke. The similarities between what has happened with the E.T. phenomenon, and the message of Clarke's book leave the enlightened

73

reader with a chilling apprehension.

The classic novel *Childhood's End* tells of an era in man's development when a race of aliens surround earth in their huge spacecraft. They bring a season of peace to mankind. Finally, after a lengthy period of time during which they keep their identity secret, the creatures land and make themselves known to gatherings of humans. These beings, called "Overlords," are warmly welcomed by two children who having run into the spacecraft later emerge with them. The following quote is taken from the book and describes the reaction of the crowd as they see the aliens for the first time:

> It was a tribute to the Overlord's psychology, and to their careful years of preparation, that only a few people fainted. Yet there could have been fewer still who did not feel the ancient terror brush for one aweful instance against their minds before reason banished it forever. There was no mistake. The leathery wings, the little horns, the barbed tail—all were there. The most terrible of legends had come to life out of the unknown past.[14]

In Clarke's story, these overlords go on to reveal man's future—a future that sees the dissolving of the human race, and its children becoming part of a cosmic "overmind."

Seeing little children 30 years after the first publishing of this book hugging E.T. dolls and singing the lyrics to a pop song that lavishes affection on this little "god" from a heavenly chariot could easily leave one wondering just what will happen to this generation of "Star Wars babies." Will they reach out and embrace the occult and become part of a system that rejects biblical truth, while all the time accepting the demonic forces that the Scriptures define as ultimately destructive to the human soul?

To many, fantasy films appear to be harmless entertainment, but when one realizes that those who craft these films are masters at their art, and have learned how to move an audience not only to wonder, but perhaps to witchcraft as well, then the greater impact of this art form comes into focus. Ingmar Bergman, one of the greatest moviemakers of all time, confirmed this by stating that films have the power to deceive.

Watching these "space operas" has become a part of American life, but how the viewer evaluates what's being preached through them is a question worthy of much thought. Youth and adults would do well not to be taken in by such illusions no matter how cutely they're packaged.

These characters represent more than exciting entertainment. They proclaim a new paganism. They display religious experiences and spiritual forces that are far more than fantasy. Behind the barrage of space-age cinematic wizardry is a clear message of the occult. Those who unknowingly swallow it will be tempted to turn away from the God of the Bible and pursue a belief system rooted in the evil spirit world.

TAKING INVENTORY

1. List some of the most recent movies you and your family have seen. The author tells us in this chapter that a clear message of the occult is evident in many of today's popular movies. Do you agree or disagree? What evidence do you have to support your answer?

2. Movie producer George Lucas has been quoted as saying *Star Wars* is his attempt to "come up with a perspective of God." How do his perspective of God and the Christian perspective of God compare? List the differences.

6
Romance

Soap Operas and Novels

Much of this book has focused on the diversions facing youth, but as we approach this next subject we'll see that the realm of secular fantasy is one that ensnares adults as well.

When it comes to TV, adults are more likely to be captivated than children. Daniel R. Anderson, a University of Massachusetts professor, has studied the TV habits of children and adults for 12 years. His research reveals that children are not as attentive to TV because they can be diverted by other activities, whereas adults have developed a skill for passive viewing.[1]

In fact, this problem can be attested to by the surfacing of such groups as "The Couch Potatoes" fraternity, a club with 5,000 members, formed interestingly enough not by children watching cartoons, but by adults "hooked" on the tube. One of the club's founders claims his 3-year-old TV has never been turned off. The champions in this club are the "superspuds" who watch five or more sets at once.[2]

Most of my pre-adolescent life was spent without a TV

in our home, but with the coming of the late '50s, our family joined millions of other Americans by placing the "electronic box" in our living room. Generations since have grown up with the TV in the center of the family's activities. The average child will watch 20,000 thirty-second commercials every year. Before most kids leave high school, they will have seen 18,000 TV murders. Now that cable TV has become available, children have the option of watching up to 100 channels.[3]

What possible effect is all this access to the imaginative world of prime time having on Americans? To discover this, perhaps we must first ask ourselves what seems to be the predominant message pouring through this medium into our living rooms? One *Washington Post* columnist seems to have nailed it down when he gave his readers the following observations:

> Sometimes when my wife and I are watching a television commercial featuring a sexy woman—posing before cars, luring us to the Caribbean ("Come to Jamaica"), pushing a soft drink or maybe a "sophisticated" bottle of wine—she asks, deadpan, "What do you think they're selling?" The answer, obviously, is sex. *Dallas,* after all, is not a show about a city and *Dynasty* is not a show about genealogy. If those shows are not about sex, then *Lassie* was not a show about a dog."[4]

In this commentator's view, certain media have a definite underlying message. Is that message getting through and changing the way millions of Americans think about life and love?

To give another example of this problem, I'm reminded of a review I read critiquing the Woody Allen film, *The Purple Rose of Cairo*. The plot of the film involves a woman during the depression era, who is caught in the humdrum of a boring life, job and marriage. She habitually attends the cinema. One day, one of the characters on screen, a dreamy movie hero, sees her sitting in the audience and steps out of the film into her life. The movie critic went on to discuss the filmmaker's unique way of commenting on how easily modern man can step in and out of his fantasies.

As silly as such a film might sound, it is probably as graphic an illustration as could be asked for in exposing some of the incredible problems facing men and women out there in the wonderland of habitual soap opera watching. Forty percent of American households with TVs are estimated to be watching at least one soap opera in any given week. Nielsen figures estimate that daytime soaps outcompete any other type of programming.

"Glamor is the rage this fall," said *Time* magazine last year when it commented on the growing popularity of nighttime "soaps."[5] And if the new season is any measure of future trends, then it looks like more of the same. More money than ever is being pumped into the productions of these elaborate programs. Twelve to fifteen new outfits are created for each episode and the glittering attractiveness of all this has created a spin-off industry where lines of clothing and jewelry are marketed to the millions who watch and long to be like the stars.

Time magazine commented that the present obsession with glamor is a renewal of the fantasy world Hollywood used to dish out 30-40 years ago. One TV executive gave his opinion on the growing interest in these types of programs:

When the biggest fear the audience has is of
somebody pressing the button and blowing the
world away, I think people want a little fantasy.
They want to escape. They want to look at beautiful women, especially when the rest of the world
isn't so beautiful to look at.[6]

In the final analysis, though, what does looking at beautiful men and women in beautiful settings, who have time to
pursue many lovers and exotic travel, do to the men and
women who faithfully watch them? These stars do more than
entertain; they actually offer strong examples to their admir-
ers.

"I feel grateful that Joan, Linda and I are role models for
women in America," says Linda Gray, star of the nighttime
soap *Dallas*. But are these role models even realistic, and if
so, are they the kind of people the world needs more of?

One writer examining the endless stream of daytime
romantic programming found the illusions they presented
hard to swallow:

Nor have I encountered all those people who talk
to themselves, usually while employing the
thousand-mile stare. Nor do I accept friends
dropping by to see each other three times a day or
the degree to which characters meddle in other
characters' lives.[7]

Even if all this did have some touch with reality, is this
the sort of example that men and women should want to
model their lives after? What does all this wide-awake
dreaming do to those who spend hours in its emotional
maze?

One study pointed out that there could be a possible link between soaps and suicide:

> The only study of soap opera available showed a several-a-day increase in the national suicide rate following soap opera suicide, the National Coalition on Television Violence said. The NCTV also noted that these programs contain "verbal threats of violence and hatred that average 13 per hour".[8]

Dealing with the normal stress of daily life in the United States would seem challenging enough, but adding to it the emotional strife of fictional characters just seems like asking for trouble. Some might argue that far from adding to the problem, soaps provide a release valve from the humdrum of daily living. A release valve is one thing, but when you consider the total involvement these programs draw from their viewers, one wonders where they are escaping to. N. Katzman, in his article on TV soap operas, gave the following estimate of their impact on watchers:

> The almost realism of the characters and themes, the repetition due to slow pace, and the extremely large numbers of hours spent viewing soap operas indicate that these shows have great potential power. They can establish or reinforce value systems. They can suggest how people should act in certain situations. They can legitimate behavior and remove taboos.[9]

If there's any question about how involved viewers can get, their responses through the mails should wipe out any doubts. One report announced that approximately one-quarter of a million birthday cards were sent to one character on *As the World Turns* who celebrated his 65th birthday. When the famous TV duo of Luke and Laura had their make-believe TV marriage, they were showered with telegrams of congratulations and even wedding presents from well-wishers. Their ceremony had more viewers than the real-life wedding of Prince Charles and Lady Diana.[10]

When TV viewers focus on the "beautiful people" the media presents to us, there is the potential for serious damage in their social and marital relationships. Studies at Arizona State and Montana State Universities presented the possibility that couples can become disappointed with the physical attractiveness of their own mates after they've been overly exposed to the model-perfect beauty of the stars.

Students in one study rated a picture of an average-looking member of the opposite sex less good-looking after they had surveyed ads in various magazines. In a similar study, participants watched the TV program "Charlie's Angels" while rating pictures of possible blind dates. Those watching the program rated the girls in the pictures less attractive than other participants who rated the same girls while watching another program. It appears that compared to the female TV stars, the blind dates came off as less attractive.[11]

Studying this same problem in the world of the soap opera fan, we find a similar result. Velma Angel, in her inciteful book on soap operas, tells of her experience with a woman struggling with the disruptive influence of soap operas on her life:

> I tried to force him [her husband] to be like the soap characters. He didn't watch the soaps, so he didn't even know what he was supposed to mea-

82

sure up to. I was dissatisfied with him. The soaps
not only hurt my marriage but they hindered my
sexual relationship with my husband. My own
husband became unattractive to me. I wanted him
to be the ultimate in romance . . . charming,
good-looking. I would pick out certain characters
and tell him, "I wish you were like this," or
"Why don't you do that?" It was a constant com-
parison. I watched soaps all day, and when he
came home there would be something wrong. I
was always upset at something he did or didn't
do.[12]

Angel goes on to relate how women experience depression, low self-esteem, anxiety and fatigue, all related to their
overwhelming fascination with the soaps. They feel cheated
because they don't have all the elegant treasures and excitement their TV heroines have. Much of this frustration ends
up being directed at their husbands and thus further damages
their marriages.

Such obsession for TV soaps tends to distort some wom-
en's perspective of the world. In an article in *U.S. News and
World Report*, this is confirmed:

Among millions of young girls who watch as
many as three soap operas a day, studies find an
exaggerated sense of the frequency of rape, pre-
marital sex and extramarital affairs. On MTV, the
portrayal of women shows the young that
"women need to be sexual to have any power at
all."[13]

Realizing that the minds behind these programs are not

83

generally the kind that are sympathetic to the stable principles that God has established for building lasting relationships, it's no wonder that so many problems erupt in a marriage where one or more of the partners is caught up in the
sensual, glittering unreal world of "Daytime Drama." Studies have shown that soap scriptwriters and editors are far
removed from the morality of the Scriptures when it comes
to their views on such things as women's rights, homosexuality and sexual standards.[14]

Following the present trend, it doesn't appear as though
TV will have an overnight change in its moral persuasion.
Considering this fact, the individual who is serious about
removing the negative influence of such emotional and mental pollution from his life would do well to exercise the ultimate in personal censorship, flip off the switch or remove
the TV from his home altogether.

Television

Television in general, as one author put it, "has become a
wasteland for Americans." A published report summarized a
12-week prime-time period when TV showed: 2,149 acts of
violence, 915 uses of profanity and 2,019 scenes of sex. The
report went on to state that: "80 percent of the allusions to
sexual intercourse in prime-time TV (in a particular year)
were depicted as being outside of marriage."[15]

Some might tend to think that most viewers can pas-
sively watch TV without any negative effects. But the mere
fact that American businesses spend over $13 billion a year
to sell their products speaks very strongly of TV's power to
influence. When the average couple spends 46 hours per
week watching TV and only 27-½ minutes talking to each
other it's easy to understand why today's marriages are
struggling.

In an April 1976, issue of *Psychology Today,* the effects TV is having on our society were discussed:

> The influence television has on the average viewer is phenomenal. Studies indicate that a heavy viewer (4 or more hours/day), generally speaking, thinks of the world as more dangerous than those who watch two hours or less. Consequently, heavy viewers are less trustful of their fellow citizens and more fearful of the real world. It has been found that violence on prime-time network TV cultivates exaggerated assumptions about the threat of danger in the real world. Fear is a universal emotion, and easy to exploit.

With the emergence of TV has come a great decline in literacy. TV viewing does not require any other physical or mental activity than to absorb what is coming through the tube. TV offers a universal curriculum that everyone and anyone can learn. Unfortunately, the major portion of this "curriculum" is unrealistic.

Take for example, the popular series, *Marcus Welby, M.D.* It is estimated that nearly 250,000 letters were sent by viewers asking "the doctor," Marcus Welby, for medical advice. And if adults can be so affected by the "reality" of TV, what kind of effect must it have on children? It is said that by the age of 10, the average youngster spends more hours a week in front of the TV screen than in the classroom."[16]

Romance Novels

Shoppers walking into the average supermarket find themselves passing book racks groaning under the weight of paperback novels, a large part of which center on one theme:

feminine fantasy. Covers with nearly naked men, passion-ately embracing starry-eyed women, whose garments appear too small to contain their overly ample mammary glands, are stacked up in displays near checkout stands where they can't be missed.

Suddenly, it seems that this feminine form of fiction is having a revival. Estimates have it that there are as many as 20 million romance readers and that they spend half-a-billion dollars on novels each year. One company alone, Harlequin Enterprises, sold 218 million romance novels in 1982.[17]

With the number of women reading these books, one wonders what draws the readers back again and again to buy the latest publication of this pulpy passion. Perhaps it's the fact that the characters in these books live the kind of excit-ing lives that the reader dreams about. One-hundred-twenty yearsago, when romantic fiction had its modern revival, the books of the day echoed the life-styles of their times. Today's readers though find a new style of heroines strolling the corridors of contemporary fiction. One article on romance novels made the following observation:

> Heroines are more sophisticated, confident and mature. They are more sexual.[18]

There's more violence in some of today's female novels, too. A professor of sociology at Hamline University in St. Paul, Minnesota, described this trend:

> As heroines get stronger, heroes get stronger. So there's stronger sexual interaction. This leads to more violence, which is incorporated into plots because it is something women have to deal with (in real life).[19]

But how much of this fiction is like real life? Often

women will read these novels hoping to dream about the perfect male companion. The heroes in these romances are different than men in real life, as the professor pointed out in one comment: "They're men as women want them to be."[20] These men don't go hunting and fishing too often. They don't spend a lot of time "out with the boys." They love animals and children, and aren't overly involved in watching sports on TV, or too busy working on cars. They seem to know the latest about women's fashions and home furnishings. These men are attractive to women, but they're *not* real.

What possible effect can these types of books have on women who immerse themselves in this make-believe world by day only to awake from it when their husbands come home from work hungry and tired at night? Somehow one feels that the false expectation built up by these fantasy images can have a damaging effect on a woman's power to deal with the reality of keeping a marriage together in the present turbulent era.

TAKING INVENTORY

1. Since the '50s, TV has become an integral part of most American homes. On the one hand, this is very beneficial; we are a much more informed nation because of this form of media. There are, however, many negative aspects to TV viewing. With your family, make a list of the benefits of TV; then beside it make a list of the negative aspects. There are many cited in this chapter. What others can you think of?

2. Romance novels are also highlighted in this chapter.

What are some of the dangers involved in being overly engrossed in novels of this sort? How are you currently balancing the kinds of reading you are doing? In other words, how much time are you spending in God's Word and in books that are edifying to the Body of Christ as opposed to books that are not?

7
Vain Imaginations

Distraction—
Deception—Degradation

In the preceding chapters we have dealt with some of the major fantasies our culture faces. Undoubtedly the reader has identified some of the dangers that involvement in these areas can have. Researching these problems has revealed that people's struggles with improper thoughts usually fall into one of three categories.

First of all, there's the potential for *distraction*. People can so actively pursue their dreams that they spend excessive amounts of time doing it.

Second, someone overly distracted by what the Bible calls "vain imaginations" (see Rom. 1:21) can fall into the trap of *deception*. Once deceived by their fantasies, individuals can actually begin to believe these false messages.

Third, there is the possibility that a person distracted and deceived by these illusions can eventually experience *degradation*. Enslavement to one's imaginations is an all-too-real problem for those addicted to this type of mental euphoria.

Distraction: Fantasy's First Danger

Tucked away in the Old Testament are certain portions of Scripture that are often left unread. Many of these accounts deal with unusual circumstances. In 1 Kings, chapter 20, there is one such interesting segment that tells the story of a prophet who went to great extremes to communicate his message.

He requested to be beaten up and then in a disheveled and wounded state placed himself along the road where the king of Israel would pass. He also carefully disguised his face with ashes. The king saw the beaten man by the side of the road and stopped to inquire about his condition. The king got the following answer and a startling rebuke from the Lord:

> Thy servant went out into the midst of the battle; and, behold, a man turned aside, and brought a man unto me, and said, Keep this man: if by any means he be missing, then shall thy life be for his life, or else thou shalt pay a talent of silver. And as thy servant was busy here and there, he was gone. And the king of Israel said unto him, So *shall* thy judgment *be; * thyself has decided *it*. And he hasted, and took the ashes away from his face; and the king of Israel discerned him that he *was* of the prophets. And he said unto him, Thus saith the LORD, because thou hastlet go out of *thy* hand a man whom I appointed to utter destruction, therefore thy life shall go for his life, and thy people for his people. And the king of Israel went to his house heavy and displeased, and came to Samaria (1 Kings 20:39-43).

There is much to learn from this passage, but one thing stands out as relevant to our study. The king had compromised himself by making a covenant with the enemy of Israel and had allowed this enemy to go free. A certain phrase the prophet gives, though, perhaps capsulizes what Ahab's real problem was: *"As thy servant was busy here and there, he was gone."* The ruler of Israel was distracted from his priority. He had allowed other things to enter into his life and thereby mar the godly judgment he so badly needed. The same is true for each of us today. We can be so busy with our "mental games" that we lose sight of our priorities and miss out on the blessings of God.

If God was your chief enemy, and you existed with a fervent passion to avenge yourself against Him, what tactic would you use to bring the greatest possible harm? Most likely, you would attack that which He loves the most, His people, knowing fully that you could never attack Him directly. This, in effect, is the ploy of Satan. His subtle plan is to distract people away from thinking about who God really is by filling their minds with those things which appeal to the natural appetites of the flesh. And one of the most effective methods he has deployed is the use of the media.

Media Addicts

American Christians are, by and large, no longer people of the Book. We have become fascinated by the visual feast offered to us every day through the mass communication network. A 1983 Nielsen finding showed that the average American home watched TV seven hours and two minutes per day.[1] Listening to pop music was another distraction that has overwhelmed many people and gobbled up their time. In interviews with youth, while covering the subject of fantasy, we discovered that it's not uncommon to find young people listening to secular rock music five hours a day.

Avid fantasy role-playing game "addicts" we interviewed could spend hours playing the game. One former Dungeon Master stated that over a period of four months, he played the game five to six days a week, 12-14 hours per day. Often he found himself becoming upset with the other players when they wanted to stop playing the game at 2 in the morning instead of 6 A.M. Obviously the massive amounts of time people spend indulging in these types of pursuits means that other areas of their lives go neglected. The most tragic neglect is that Americans have stopped reading the Bible.

Dusty Bibles

In surveys while speaking to various groups, I've been shocked to discover how few people have read the entire Bible through one time. It's estimated that the average reader is capable of reading the Scriptures through in a total of 70 hours. If the normal TV watcher substitutes just 10 days of his visual media diet with Scripture reading, he could read through the whole Bible. Even for a slow reader, it shouldn't take more than 20 days.

When all the hours we've spent watching TV are totalled up against those we have spent in God's Word, I'm sure most of us will stand guilty of allowing this electronic distraction to rob us of one of the most important priorities in our lives. Jesus wisely stated, "Man shall not live by bread alone, but by every word that proceedeth out of the mouth of God" (Matt. 4:4). The "bread" of TV is a poor substitute for the "bread" of life.

Physically, Americans are some of the best-fed people in the world. Yet spiritually we're some of the most anemic. A hunger for the Word of the Lord has been replaced with a fascination with entertainment. God doesn't expect us to become reclusive and sit in little chambers reading the Bible all day, but certainly the balance that measures our spiritual health shows a drastic tilt to the wrong side. We would do well to put into practice the words of the psalmist who spoke of the happy condition of the person who meditates in God's Word day and night (see Ps. 1:2).

The words of Jeremiah echo what should be our true longing:

> Thy words were found, and I did eat them; and thy word was unto me the joy and rejoicing of mine heart: for I am called by thy name, O LORD God of hosts (Jer. 15:16).

Jeremiah, like Job, had esteemed God's Word more important than his necessary food (see Job 23:12). Often a child left to his own way can become so jaded by his consumption of candy that wholesome food no longer is appealing. Is it possible that we have become so satiated with the food of the entertainment industry that "God's dinners" no longer interest us?

Pay TV or Pray to Thee

Another vast area of neglect is prayer. The closets of intercession are empty while our family rooms fill up with new and interesting electronic gadgets. We have linked up by cable with all the channels we can handle but have left closed the one linkup that brings life. People who used to listen for God's still small voice, now drown it out with the deafening blast of pop tunes.

A few years ago, while I was on staff at a large church in Sacramento, a guest speaker jolted our congregation with an amazing claim. This man, who was the pastor of one of the nation's largest churches, said that in his travels throughout the states, he had been surveying various congregations to discover how much they really prayed. He was sadly amazed to discover that very few prayed more than 10 minutes a day. Now, God's not looking for mindless drones that will chant meaningless prayers for hours on end. But God does long for meaningful fellowship with His people; the kind of fellowship that comes when we're willing to spend time alone with Him to really come to know Him. He is our heavenly Bridegroom and we are His bride.

Of what little I've learned about marriage, after 17 happy years with the same lovely woman, one thing is certain: Communication is one of the greatest keys to keeping love alive. I know without asking that my wife would never be satisfied if all I spent with her was a mere 10 minutes a day. Yet, somehow we think that we can really come to know God by spending a few minutes in His presence and then wandering away to spend hours distracted by our fantasies.

Deception

The second risk people take when they fool around in the fantasy zone is the possibility of being deceived. There's no doubt that many of the subjects we have covered earlier in this book are fascinating and pleasurable. This is what makes them so dangerous. It's the rare person who runs off pursuing something that brings them pain.

The Scriptures point out the excitement that selfish pleasure-seeking will bring, but they're also careful to stress that these joys are only temporary (see Heb. 11:25). Part of the devil's trap is to create a world of sensual and mental euphoria only to later spring it closed on the unsuspecting. A

94

person fascinated with fantasy films or the flashing images of rock videos is, more than likely, being set up.

Fantasy Leads to a Death Plunge

Several years ago, when I was a young minister, I worked with many people who came out of the drug culture. One of these was a young man who had a powerful conversion. After his conversion, he shared with me the tragic but true story of a former companion who failed to make it out of the drug scene alive.

One day, the two of them had taken hallucinogenic drugs while they sat on the edge of a canyon. As the ecstatic effects of the drug began to work on their minds, an apparent state of bliss enveloped them. Suddenly, the young man's friend stood to his feet and did a perfect dive off the edge of the cliff. A few moments later, his life was crushed out on the rocks below.

This gruesome story illustrates what is happening to millions who have been deceived by fantasy's allurement. Reviewing the story with me later, the young man speculated that perhaps his friend had seen some imaginary pool of cosmic light and plunged in for a blissful swim, only to discover moments later that his senses had tricked him.

My heart goes out to that young man as it does to a whole generation who have opened their minds to the deceptions of Satan. In a similar way many of the fantasies parading before us today may be illusions that will lead to death.

The prince of darkness has transformed himself into an angel of light (see 2 Cor. 11:14). And he's not putting out his wares without the necessary garnish that will make them appealing. But beware, because for the person who chooses to toy with the devil's delusions, the consequences can be eternal.

What would the young people who have taken their lives after being overcome with bondage to Dungeons and Dragons® say to us if we could hear them now? What sad statements does the list of those who've overdosed on drugs make when you think of the rock lyrics that glorify cocaine and heroin? And who cries for the young girl who, after her third abortion, can't live with the guilt any longer? Her superstar movie heroes have made casual sex look like harmless fun. Perhaps now she's beginning to understand that fantasy can also deceive.

Degradation: Fantasy's Final Danger

Addiction to fantasy "mind-fixing" eventually leads to total enslavement. It's interesting how clear the Bible is when it comes to this area of our thought life. God understands better than anyone how the dynamics of the human mind and emotions work and how the unbridled chasing after our perverted thoughts can eventually leave us helpless servants to lifeless images.

The Secret Room of Abomination

One day God gave the ancient prophet Ezekiel a frightening tour of the Temple and the hideous perversions that were taking place in it.

God showed him not only the open idolatry that was taking place in the Temple, but also the secret idol worship that occurred in what the King James Version of the Bible phrases as "the chamber of imagery." This hidden room contained paintings of grotesque creatures that the elders secretly burned incense to (see Ezek. 8:5-12).

Today, God's temple is our body (see 1 Cor. 6:19,20), and although no idol may be found in the public part of our lives, what about our "chamber of imagery"? What goes on beyond this hidden door that leads to our minds? What possible images are portrayed there? The most tragic thing about the elders' secret room was that they had made it a place of worship. The incense filling the chamber of imagery was a symbol of worship. Plainly stated, worship is giving one's affection to something or someone they consider God.

How often today are people quietly, but fully, giving their affections to some secret fantasy playing itself out on a hidden screen in their daydreams? Although we can convince ourselves that it's all in secret and that no one knows, our loving heavenly Father knows, and it breaks His heart. Although there are several potential problems related to inner idolatry, two glaring areas tend to stand out: sexual fantasy and romantic fantasy.

Sexual Fantasy

The area of sexual fantasy tends to plague men mostly, but with the growing distribution of slick soft-core porn magazines and videos, it has become a problem for women, too. Purveyors of video perversion are adding more detailed plots and romance to their films in hopes of pulling in the women's market.

Sexual fantasy was an area that Jesus addressed frankly:

> But I say unto you, That whosoever looketh on a
> woman to lust after her hath committed adultery
> with her already in his heart (Matt. 5:28).

More than likely His listeners had previously thought adultery only involved a physical act, yet it's clear that Jesus considered our thought life subject to the laws of God as well. A person that allows their mind to drift into areas of perverted thinking is going to find a continuing struggle with the desire to give in to their fantasies.

The ancient prophet Samuel records the story of King David's tragic fall into adultery. This sad chapter in his life is evidence of the potential danger of allowing our thoughts to bring us into sin (see 2 Sam. 11:1-4).

This segment of Scripture begins by showing David in what appears to be a state of boredom and idleness. His armies are off to war and he is in the palace with time on his hands. Certainly one of the dangers of idleness is its potential to create an atmosphere where we look for the wrong distractions to keep us occupied.

Such was the case with the "sweet singer of Israel." Discovering a naked woman in your view is no sin when you're not responsible for her being there, but allowing one's gaze to dwell on the scene is an open invitation to lust. Whereas women find touch or tender words more of an initial part of sexual response, generally speaking, men are first stimulated sexually by sight.

None of us can be certain what went on in David's mind as he looked down on the exposed intimate beauty of Bathsheba, but I'm sure most men would agree that soon their thoughts would turn from a merely asthetic appreciation of the female form to the strong desire to possess the object of attraction. Simply put, David saw Bathsheba, his imagination portrayed the pleasant option of exploring the possibilities further and it was only a matter of time before the two were in bed together living out what began as a simple look in the wrong direction.

Looking in the wrong direction is something that men are being tempted to do today more powerfully than in any previous generation. With the availability of pornography, the open display of half-dressed and seductively posed female flesh in magazine ads and on TV, and the lessened moral restraints brought on by the so-called sexual revolution, the average male can find almost unlimited possibilities for sexual sin. The important thing to remember is that it all begins in the mind. A thought life out of control will ultimately lead to some form of outward sin.

And what of the sin of adultery? Some say it's really not a crime, that no one's hurt when two consenting adults decide they want to enjoy a sexual adventure outside of the covenant of marriage. There are those who would rationalize that so long as their affair is kept secret from their mates, it will not hurt their marriage. In fact, some have even counseled that such interludes can put a new spark back into a dead marriage. The tragedy of all this thinking is that none of us can live a double life for long without our belief systems sounding the kind of alarm that will only go away by battering at our consciences until they are permanently damaged.

> Speaking lies in hypocrisy; having their conscience seared with a hot iron (1 Tim. 4:2).

Our inner psychological make-up is as complex as the details of our outward human body. Damaging our personality can be just as potentially wounding as a cut, gunshot or blow to our flesh and bones. The book of Proverbs and 1 Peter both give us strong warnings about the destructive force of uncontrolled immoral passion.

> Dearly beloved, I beseech *you* as strangers and pilgrims, abstain from fleshly lusts, which war against the soul (1 Pet. 2:11).

> *But* whoso committeth adultery with a woman

99

lacketh understanding: he *that* doeth it destroyeth
his own soul (Prov. 6:32).

What does it mean to war against or destroy our own
soul? First of all, it's necessary to clarify the nature of the
soul. In 1 Thessalonians 5:23, Paul outlines man's triune
nature: body, soul and spirit. The body, the outward part of
man, is easily defined. The spirit, although more mysteri-
ous, can be described as that deepest inward part of the
human make-up where God touches and communicates with
us. That leaves the soul. What remains are the elements that
produce our personality, mind, will and emotions. It is these
three factors that are disturbed when people allow their sexual drives to run unchecked outside of God's boundaries.

Let me carefully interject here that sex is God's idea and
as long as it remains within the safe boundaries of marriage
it becomes a glorious and creative expression of human love.
But once removed from those protective walls, it becomes as
destructive as a wildfire.

Perhaps one of the most graphic illustrations of this is the
tragic story of a young man who murdered his girlfriend in a
small town in California. At the time, I lived in a larger city
nearby and read the story in the paper after its disruptive
force shook the little community where this crime had
occurred.

The young man and his girlfriend had become sexually
intimate. Then one day he was informed by her that she was
no longer seriously interested in their relationship. This was
too much for the broken-hearted lover to bear. He told his
friends that he was going to kill the girl who had jilted him.

Undoubtedly the thought of anyone else possessing her
was tormenting him. He went to her house with a loaded pis-
tol and took her life. When the police arrived they found a

dead girl and a broken young man who confessed his tragic plight. "All she wanted me for was sex," were his words. Too late, he came to realize that intimacy without the commitment and trust of marriage can rip apart the mind and emotions as surely as the bullets from his gun had torn the flesh of his slain lover.

Although all broken love affairs do not end like this one, there are millions of individuals who carry similar wounds. These inner hurts can leave people with crippled personalities. All too often, these mental and emotional scars keep them from ever building healthy relationships. Outside of God restoring love, a person betrayed will find it hard to trust and give themselves to others.

And for those who have betrayed others through selfish sexual pursuits, a hardened heart and ruined conscience will find guilt and callousness keeping them from blooming to full potential. All we have to do is count the number of shattered marriages, broken-hearted children and disjointed social structures of our day to see the destructive force of sexual fantasy and ultimately sexual sin.

Romantic Fantasy

As tempting as the present wave of pornography is for men, there is perhaps an even more alluring wave of degradation invading the world of women in our culture. Ever since the birth of romanticism in the Middle Ages, the knight-in-shining-armor syndrome has been part of our Western culture. Every healthy marriage has romance in it. Candlelight and love notes, flowers and special weekends together away from the humdrum of the work-a-day world can keep a spark in marriage. Daily acts of kindness and tender affection keep love alive and well.

But when I address the subject of romantic fantasy in the

101

following context, I'm addressing a problem that has become more than a mere distraction. Millions of American women have found it an addictive and alluring problem, short-circuiting their proper desires and leading them astray. As the earlier chapter on soaps and romantic novels pointed out, we are being inundated with a flood of programs and literature that offers temptations many women aren't properly dealing with.

The desire to break out of the tedium of the familiar is a common struggle for men and women alike. For women, this desire expresses itself in the realm of the romantic.

Some might object that such temporary diversions are not sinful and therefore not that bad. They're only temporary playgrounds for a bored mind. Yet, there is clear evidence from Scripture, and experience, to prove otherwise.

Thousands of years ago, the prophet Ezekiel proclaimed the sad message of the unfaithfulness of God's people. To do this he used the analogy of two sisters who represent the now divided kingdom of Israel and Judah. One sister, Aholah, was symbolic of Samaria, the primary city of Israel. The other, Aholibah, stood for Jerusalem, the capital of Judah. Aholah had become promiscuous and pursued strange lovers. Her sister, seeing Aholah's escapades, followed in her footsteps with even more enthusiasm. After seeing billboard-size pictures of the finely dressed princes of Babylon, Aholibah became completely enamored with them. Her inordinate affection ultimately resulted in a series of sexual encounters that left her morally polluted (see Ezek. 23:11-17).

As we look at Aholibah's demise, we see she began her misadventure by gazing at the paintings of handsome men and then dreaming of future encounters with them. It wasn't long until her messengers had gone out and called these men to join her in a bed of adultery. What began as a longing look soon became a passion that drove her to perversion.

Often women who fall into immoral affairs or fornication never intend things to work out the way they do. Yet somehow or another, a situation comes along that allows them to fall into temptation and sin. A woman who is constantly fantasizing will also be a woman who is sending out messages.

A close friend of mine, a minister to youth, had a concerned young woman come to him for counseling. She asked him why every young man who took her out wanted to take things "all the way." It seemed that these boys were not content merely to date her; they wanted a sexual relationship as well.

As my friend talked with the troubled girl, he soon realized that her dress and sensual manner sent out a clear "message." Even though she verbalized to these young men she didn't want that type of relationship, her personal appearance and attitude told them otherwise. A mind that dwells on romance is also one that tends to send out a romantic signal. It may only be subconsciously, but eventually someone will read the message and "come to call."

Isn't the vicarious enjoyment of an illicit passionate account, whether in a book or movie, also a form of adultery in the mind? And once it's begun in the mind, how long will it be until it's outwardly expressed? Worldly fantasy ultimately will bring such degradation.

This chapter could be the last in this book if it weren't for the wonderful love and grace of our heavenly Father who can lift us above the destructive fantasies and passions that seek to enslave us. Scripture not only gives us the clear promise of power over our circumstances, but also a solution that provides us a positive channel for the creative side of our imaginations.

TAKING INVENTORY

1. The author makes the observation that Americans today are neglecting their Bibles. How much time do you and your family members spend in God's Word on a daily basis? Have you read the Bible clear through? If not, would you be willing to make a commitment with your family to do so, either on an individual basis or with each other?

2. Prayer is also a neglected area in many of our lives today. Do you and your family members (alone or together) spend time each day in prayer with your heavenly Father? There are many devotionals and study plans on the market that are helpful in creating and enriching personal and family prayer time. Check with your church or local Christian bookstore.

8
Dealing with Fantasy

Identification—
Eradication

In the preceding chapters we have tried to point out some of the growing areas of mental abuse in our present-day, media-soaked culture. No doubt as technology continues to improve in its ability to imitate and enhance life, new forms of sensual temptation will flow into our culture. This is all the more reason for Christians to learn to deal more effectively with the world of fantasy. Honestly facing up to the problems of our society can be sobering and a bit discouraging. Nonetheless, Christians must be open about the situation if we are to develop a strategy to overcome it.

Concerned citizens groups across America are rising up in an attempt to put an end to many of the destructive media forces flooding our world. I heartily support their efforts and pray for their success. Yet, dealing with these issues on the public level is only part of the answer. There must also be a clear plan to help each person face and overcome the subtle forces of fantasy on an individual level as well.

In the following two chapters, we will deal with the

scriptural guidelines God has given us for handling vain imaginations. These principles can be summed up in three words: identification, eradication and illumination.

Identification

It's been estimated that over 1,400 advertising messages a day flood into our minds. Studies also show that by the time the average teenager graduates from high school, he will have watched approximately 22,000 hours of TV.[1] Add to that the fact that the amount of knowledge available to man will soon be doubling almost weekly.

Trying to handle all these images that tumble in front of our eyes is no small task. Yet one comforting thought is the fact that for all this information to actually lodge itself in our consciousnesses and begin to effect us, it must first pass through our eye gates and the door of our wills. Identifying these images for what they are and relegating them to their proper place is half the battle. Often people are overcome by seductive messages in the media, simply because they have failed to identify them properly and deal with them appropriately.

A couple of years ago, when my wife and I were involved in directing a Bible college, we were confronted with a situation that deeply troubled us. We happened to be talking with a very sweet girl who had been through our classes. She understood what godliness was all about and, no doubt, would have declared her strong commitment to Christ if asked about her faith.

This dear girl had just viewed a film that portrayed a very subtle message of rebellion and sensuality. The heroes in this film were a pastor's daughter, who was given to violence and fornication, and her rebel boyfriend. Through the crafty screenwriting, seductive music and colorful camera work, the filmmakers were able to portray the pastor as an uncaring stick-in-the-mud, while making the daughter and her boyfriend to be heroes.

As I talked with this former student, I realized that she had been totally taken in by the subtle seduction of this film. She had sided with the rebels and written off the pastor. No doubt, pastors aren't perfect and this one had a serious communication problem with his daughter. Nonetheless, the overall effect of the film seemed to cast the concept of moral restraint in a negative light and revelled in the idea that rebellious youth are the real heroes in the clash between the generations.

This particular situation has made me realize that sincere people often can accept the wrong message if it comes across on the right level. Looking back on our conversation, I can see that the young woman was reacting to the film primarily on an emotional level and not really evaluating all the other aspects of what the story was saying. She had identified with the main characters' struggles that were portrayed as virtuous, and then rejoiced in their apparent triumph over the supposed negative influence of the older generation. This is often the case with fantasy's deceptive appeal. Somehow we're made to think that if it feels, sounds or looks good, how can it be otherwise.

A Word from Our Sponsor

Many of these alluring messages come to us through commercials. These well-thought-out ads pack a real punch that can grab us before we realize what they're really saying. I've torn a series of ads from a few secular news magazines as a point of illustration. The first one shows a couple, elegantly dressed, dining at a nicely appointed table spread in a field of wild flowers. In the distance, snow-capped mountains rise up to meet puffy clouds caught in the shades of a purple sunset. It's a very romantic setting. Parked nearby, in clear view, is the main attraction—a truck. The real point of the ad is to sell you an automobile. Yet to sell you the truck, the company first has to sell you a little romance. They appear to be saying, if you have the truck you can also have an ecstatic love relationship.

The next example shows a beautiful model in a glittering evening dress. She has one leg seductively draped around a cigarette carton that's nearly as tall as she is. The "come hither" look on her face seems to portray not only feminine allurement, but a sense that this woman has it altogether. The long cigarette jutting up between her fingers makes it clear she's a smoker. Her sophistication makes it clear she's the kind of woman others would like to imitate. This tobacco company knows what it's doing. They're not only selling cigarettes, they're selling the idea that if you buy their brand you may also gain a little sex appeal and confidence in the deal.

Another printed commercial uses two very attractive models, male and female, to pitch its particular brand of liquor. Sitting by a swimming pool in a dreamily lit set, the couple, sexily clad in bathing suits, are breaking the ice over two glasses of smooth-looking booze. Their provocative smiles and "perfect" bodies say a lot more than "buy our alcohol." The whole scene has the appearance of youthfulness, beauty, romantic intrigue and sensuality. It seems to say you can be one of the beautiful people by merely taking a few sips of the right drink.

Ad agencies aren't dumb. They make their money by selling their clients' products. They've spent countless hours studying the forces that make people buy. It's apparent from the type of ads that continue to crop up in magazines and on

TV that one of the best ways to sell a product is to sell fantasy along with it. The founder of Soloflex, a state-of-the-art exercise weight machine, said this about using sexual teases in their ads:

> There's no way I can sell the product without selling sex.[2]

Whether it's through films or ads, these kinds of messages are constantly going to confront the media-weary consumers of twentieth-century America.

The person who is seriously considering conquering the dangers these fantasies bring into their life would do well to carefully identify the images that flash by them and reject the ones that are improper. Proverbs 22:3 suggests the value of discerning the potential evil of a situation ahead of time.

> A prudent *man* foreseeth the evil, and hideth himself: but the simple pass on, and are punished.

By not evaluating and identifying the dangers of the thoughts that attempt to penetrate our minds, we are opening ourselves up to a whole host of mental conflicts. Each of us sits at the gateway to our minds. If we choose we can turn aside the improper thoughts. But first we must know they're improper.

One of the best examples of this principle is an experience a friend of mine had as a young man. He lived in the nation of New Zealand, a country with about 3 million people and nearly 70 million sheep. At a certain time each year, shepherds around the land would gather their sheep for shearing and branding. At the various locations, sheep dogs, barking and nipping at the sheep, would gather a great tide of white, bleating livestock and guide them like a flood down the hillsides to be funneled through a single gate.

At this gate sat a young man who had the responsibility of separating the young lambs out for branding. As each sheep bolted through the passage, he would *identify* it. If it was a lamb, the lever would be moved to one side and the tiny animal would be escorted into a holding pen where it would have its owner's identifying mark placed on it. If a grown sheep came through the chute, the lever would be moved to allow passage through to the other side, neatly guiding the furry creature to the waiting shearers.

In a similar manner, each of us has the opportunity to open and close the tunnel into the inner world of our mind. The mere flick of a "lever" can't guide away the wrong thoughts. We must be careful to evaluate each image. Don't merely accept them because they're there. Rather, be alert and watch:

> Therefore let us not sleep, as do others; but let us
> watch and be sober. For they that sleep sleep in
> the night; and they that be drunken are drunken in
> the night. But let us, who are of the day, be sober,
> putting on the breastplate of faith and love; and
> for an helmet, the hope of salvation (1 Thess.
> 5:6-8).

Putting on the helmet of salvation is a conscious choice to deflect the destructive darts that come against our minds.

Eradication

Once a wrong image or thought has been identified, the next step is to quickly deal with it. Erasing the evil picture from our thoughts is something God gives every Christian

110

the power to do. There are actually two stages to this part of the principle. One involves the removing of potential sources of temptation and the other the practical steps to deal with unavoidable thought pictures that cross our paths.

Fleeing Temptations

The psalmist understood the importance of fleeing temptation. In Psalm 101:3, we see his commitment to avoiding the circumstances for potential distraction:

I will set no wicked thing before mine eyes.

Paul exhorted the Philippians in chapter 4:8,9 to focus on the kind of thoughts that are godly:

Finally, brethren, whatsoever things are true, whatsoever things *are* honest, whatsoever things *are* just, whatsoever things *are* pure, whatsoever things *are* lovely, whatsoever things *are* of good report; if *there be* any virtue, and if *there be* any praise, think on these things. Those things, which ye have both learned, and received, and heard, and seen in me, do: and the God of peace shall be with you.

Half the battle is to cast aside these wrong images and replace them with godly ones. The Apostle instructed the church to remember and think about the Christlike qualities they had seen in his own life.

People struggling with an excessive assault of unwholesome images in their minds would do well to consider the possible source. Perhaps the wrong book or magazine needs to be tossed out. A record with questionable lyrics can easily be dumped in the trash. This author would suggest to the excessive TV viewer the wisdom of putting the TV in the closet or removing it from the house altogether if the urge to watch it is uncontrollable.

Sometimes it seems that the onslaught of tempting images are poured out in front of us with relentless efficiency. At such times, it's important to remember Christ's words. Jesus gave His disciples a prayer that established a pattern for all their prayers. One outstanding concept from the Lord's Prayer comes clearly to mind at this point:

Lead us not into temptation(Matt. 6:13).

We can claim this as a promise for deliverance from overwhelming temptation.

Even when all known allurements are removed, the sincere Christian can still be tormented by unwanted mental pictures. Satan will gather from our past experiences and daily circumstances wrong images to pull our thoughts away from the pure and lovely. To the person not instructed in the Scriptures, this assault can be demoralizing. Grappling with unwanted thoughts can appear to be a struggle without a solution. Yet, the Scriptures make it clear that God has given us all the tools we need to deal with the situation.

For the weapons of our warfare *are* not carnal but mighty in God for pulling down strongholds, casting down arguments and every high thing that exalts itself against the knowledge of God, bringing every thought into captivity to the obedience of Christ (2 Cor. 10:4,5, *NKJV*).

Paul makes it clear that as Christians we have the power

to bring our thoughts captive. The reader might say that's great, but how? How does one cleanse one's mind from these unclean thoughts and images?

In Paul's letter to the Ephesians (5:25,26), he gives us a clue as to the proper agent of cleansing:

> Husbands, love your wives, just as Christ also loved the church and gave Himself for it, that He might sanctify and cleanse it with the washing of water by the word (NKJV).

Christ loves His Church even as a husband loves his wife. His desire for us is that our lives will be pure and wholesome and He has given us His Word as the "heavenly soap" to wash out our minds.

The ancient priest under the old covenant experienced two kinds of cleansing. The first was the offering for sin that came through the sacrificial blood of animals on the altar. (This cleansing was only symbolic of the perfect cleansing Christ's blood would bring.) The second was the cleansing of their bodies as they washed in the basins made from the mirrors of the Israelite women.

Even so today, we have two kinds of cleansing. The first cleansing comes through the blood of Christ that washes away our sins and the second is the cleansing of our minds through God's Word. Even as the priest washed in a basin made of mirrors, so God's Word is like a mirror reflecting God's true picture of reality to us.

> But be doers of the word, and not hearers only, deceiving yourselves. For if anyone is a hearer of the word and not a doer, he is like a man observing his natural face in a mirror; for he observes

113

himself, goes away, and immediately forgets what kind of man he was. But he who looks into the perfect law of liberty and continues in it, and is not a forgetful hearer but a doer of the work, this one will be blessed in what he does (Jas. 1:22-25, *NKJV*).

A good daily bath in God's Word is one of the best solutions to a troubled mind. Still, some might say, how do I deal with persistent and tormenting thoughts? Once again, we can go to the Scriptures for our answers.

Jesus Himself was not without temptation:

Seeing then that we have a great High Priest who has passed through the heavens, Jesus the Son of God, let us hold fast *our* confession. For we do not have a High Priest who cannot sympathize with our weaknesses, but was in all *points* tempted as *we are, yet* without sin (Heb. 4:14,15, *NKVJ*).

In spite of our own Saviour's struggles with improper thoughts, He never once sinned. We have a graphic picture of Christ's battle and victory with temptation in Matthew 4:1-11. In this segment of Scripture we see how each time Jesus was confronted with a deceptive thought He resisted and overcame it by quoting Scripture to refute it. One phrase is repeated by Jesus three times: the simple statement, "It is written" (vv. 4,6,7).

Christ, who grew in wisdom from the days of His childhood until He became a man, had studied and memorized the Scriptures. In His hour of need He was able to wield them like a mighty sword to drive off the attack of false thoughts Satan attempted to force upon Him. The Christian, too, has a powerful weapon in the sword of the Spirit, the Word of God (see Eph. 6:17). God has given us His promise that if we submit ourselves to Him and resist the devil, he will flee from us (see Jas. 4:7).

Often, Christians will start out with good intentions, putting these principles into practice only to be defeated in their thought life by old habit patterns. Even in this seemingly impossible situation, God has given us the promise of His Word.

> No temptation has overtaken you except such as is common to man; but God *is* faithful, who will not allow you to be tempted beyond what you are able, but with the temptation will also make the way of escape, that you will be able to bear *it* (1 Cor. 10:13, *NKJV*).

There is a way out of our situations. The old habit patterns of improper thinking can be broken by establishing new ones. Consistent assaults on the strongholds Satan has built in the mind will eventually bring the old habit patterns down. Persistence and faith will pay off.

Paul wrote to his young charge Timothy the following admonition:

> Exercise thyself . . . unto godliness (1 Tim. 4:7).

This word *exercise* speaks of training, of discipline. The mind can be trained to think in new and positive ways. Practice makes perfect; persistence pays off.

I'm reminded of my son's attempts to master bicycle riding. Some children will use training wheels to hold them up until they've gained the needed balance to ride. My son decided to forget the training wheels and just "go for it." I can remember running alongside him holding the bike steady while he peddled. When he felt he was ready, he gave the word for me to let go. He set off with great determination, but a few feet later collapsed in a heap. As he picked himself up, there was no defeat in his eyes, only the determination to give it another try. And so it went until after 20 minutes of "ups and downs," he was gliding down the street like an old pro.

A Christian who practices the principles of overcoming temptation through faith in God's promises will soon find new and permanent thought patterns replacing the old ones. Submitting to God and resisting Satan with the Word will bring victory:

> For whatever is born of God overcomes the world. And this is the victory that has overcome the world—our faith. Who is he who overcomes the world, but he who believes that Jesus is the Son of God? (1 John 5:4,5, *NKJV*).

One final principle remains in our lesson on dealing with fantasy and we have given the next chapter in its entirety to the discussion of this most needed truth: Illumination.

TAKING INVENTORY

1. Before we can deal with the world of fantasy, we must be

able to identify it. In other words, what is fantasy and what is reality? The author tells us we cannot merely accept an image just because it presents itself in front of us. We are admonished to make a choice as to what we allow to pass through the gates of our eyes, ears and minds and thereby influence us. Next we must make a conscious effort to cast aside wrong images and replace them with godly ones. It would do readers well to commit to memory Philippians 4:8,9.

2. We are reminded that Jesus was not without temptation, yet He was without sin (see Heb. 4:15,16). How can Christians allow this knowledge of our Lord and Saviour to minister hope and encouragement in facing temptations before us every day?

3. God has not only given us the prayer to pray, but the promise to shield us from those things that seek to destroy us. What promise does our author remind us of for deliverance from overwhelming temptations? See the Lord's Prayer, especially the verse: "Lead us not into temptation" (Matt. 6:13).

9
Dreaming God's Dream
Creative Imaginations

Leo Szilard, father of the atom bomb, was standing on a street corner in London one day when the idea for nuclear fission entered his conscious mind. The seedbed from which this idea came was the fictional writings of H.G. Wells. Wells had been one of the great futurists of the early twentieth century. His dreams and visions, many of which are unbiblical and humanistic, nonetheless affected future generations. His novels spoke of future worlds filled with the kinds of wonders we now take for granted.

He dreamed of futuristic cities, missiles that would reach the moon and, yes, bombs made by splitting the elements. This concept had been grafted into Szilard's thinking through his reading and became part of this great physicist's pool of mental resources as he began to speculate about the possible future of nuclear research. Dreaming was part of his creative approach to science.

No doubt, God has given man the power to dream, as well as the ability to bring those dreams into reality (see

Gen. 11:6). Yet when we talk about illumination, we shouldn't just discuss man's ability to envision, but also God's ability to reveal to man His wisdom and beauty.

As far back as Genesis we see God inspiring His children to dream of future possibilities. God took Abraham out under the stars and used those countless points of light to help the patriarch visualize His promises to him. In Psalm 8, David's mind appears to be exploding as he considers the vastness of God's creation, and therefore the even greater nature of the One who spoke it into existence. It's this contemplation of the eternal that often needs the assistance of the imaginative part of man's thinking ability. It's this same area that is also the source of presumption and idolatry.

Visualization

Today, many teach a concept known as visualization. Some speculate that this technique of conceiving certain desired goals and then focusing the mind's attention upon these goals to achieve them is actually a God-given ability and can be used with His blessing. Focusing on a purpose, setting a goal and working toward its fulfillment isn't wrong. Yet there are serious concerns being voiced over the use of this principle.

In an attempt to heal inward hurts, Christians have been instructed to imagine Jesus walking into their lives and touching that wounded spot with His healing. On the surface, this concept may sound like a helpful idea. But in reality, it has the possibility for tremendous error.

First of all, we don't need an imaginary Jesus walking into our lives when we can have the real Jesus through His Holy Spirit touching our inward wounds with His love and healing (see 1 John 4:18). Second, to presume that by merely imagining this occurrence it will somehow happen is

119

in direct contradiction to the teaching of Scripture that promises that God will respond to the faith and prayers of Christians who believe and trust in the God of the unseen.

> Blessed *are* they that have not seen, and *yet* have believed (John 20:29).

> Trust in the Lord with all thine heart; and lean not unto thine own understanding. In all thy ways acknowledge him, and he shall direct thy paths (Prov. 3:5,6).

God has instructed us to walk by faith and not by sight. Third, there is the problem of creating a limited picture of God when He longs to reveal His greatness to us.

Three Sources for Ideas

There are three sources for ideas and images. One source is man's mind and heart. In this realm, man can manipulate knowledge, wisdom and information. His imagination can paint pictures on the screen of his mind and allow these images to evolve into tangible works in the real world. It would be a mistake, though, to ascribe God's inspiration or endorsement of them merely because we have used religious settings or concepts in putting them together.

Another source for ideas is the demonic realm. Satan can inject his subtle images, some even masquerading as religious, into our streams of consciousness and thereby carry us away into a dream world that brings bondage and deception.

God also works in this realm, but we must remember that when He does these dreams and images will always match up exactly with the principles and laws of Scripture. In fact, God exhorts us through Paul's Epistles to the Ephesians and Colossians that we should allow His Holy Spirit to focus our minds on the heavenly dimension:

> That the God of our Lord Jesus Christ, the Father of glory, may give unto you the spirit of wisdom and revelation in the knowledge of him: The eyes of your understanding being enlightened (Eph. 1:17,18).

> If ye then be risen with Christ, seek those things which are above, where Christ sitteth on the right hand of God. Set your affection on things above, not on things on the earth (Col. 3:1,2).

It's in such a state that God not only reveals His personal majesty to us, but also His purposes for our lives.

Perhaps one of the greatest tools in shedding the influence of worldly fantasy is to have our minds filled with the wonder of Christ's character and the unfolding purpose He has for each of us. A person whose imagination has been inspired by God is a person who has seen a reality that makes the images of fleshly fantasy appear as they truly are: empty lies.

At various points in biblical history, we can see examples of where God touched the creative force of man's imagination and unlocked it for His purposes.

God instructed Moses, according to Exodus, to build a holy tent of meeting. This place was to be the earthly residence of God's glory and presence. The unique design of the Tabernacle displays not only the practical aspects of a residence that had to be versatile and movable, but also beautiful enough to represent the glory of the eternal God. God gave Moses the blueprint, but He also gave him two helpers in whose hearts He had placed a creative skill to shape the details of this beautiful sanctuary.

It would seem improper to imagine that God simply operated these men like automatons, never allowing them to add any of their own creative ideas to the process. God had given exact instructions to the size of each object in the Tabernacle, but there is no record that He told these craftsmen exactly how the details should be shaped. When He instructed them to design angels to rest above the mercy seat of the ark, where did these images come from? Perhaps much of this was left up to their own imagination. Perhaps He unlocked their imaginations to become a direct channel for His creative force.

Just exactly where we can draw the line between godly inspiration and human creativity seems to remain a mystery. Yet, any godly sensitive artist has enough wisdom to recognize that all of these gifts come from God, and He deserves the glory.

Music

David, the sweet singer of Israel, wrote songs that have endured for ages. Should we presume that it was actually God who composed these songs and that David was merely the channel? Or is there not another picture of God's heart, a heart that looks for His creatures to respond with their own songs, inspired by His beauty, but never simply a repeating of His own invention? Somehow, we see emerging the picture of a God who gives His people talents and imagination, and then mysteriously touches that gift to give it a certain essence that marks it as heavenly.

Musical Instruments

In 1 Chronicles, we read of David's invention of musical instruments for praise. Although there were undoubtedly musical devices already in existence at that time, it appears that David sought to produce a new type of instrument that would be consecrated specifically for the purpose of worship. Creating a new sound and experimenting with scales and tonality was certainly part of David's life. God had given David an inborn talent for music, and surely He must have enjoyed watching as David used his imagination and skill to perfect a method for communicating his love back to God. Creating new yet scriptural methods of worship and proclamation obviously received God's approval. Even so today, as we open our hearts to God and allow His inspiration to mingle with a sanctified imagination, we can discover new and creative ways to serve and glorify Him.

Vision: A Last Days' Phenomenon

In Acts 2:17, the apostle Peter spoke of the end times when God would pour out His Spirit on all flesh. Part of this great spiritual awakening was to be the manifestation of dreams and visions. Throughout Scripture, various types of visions were given to God's people. Some were "open" visions where the heavenly picture enveloped the sight of the viewer and completely enclosed him. At other times, visions have been seen as an inner form of inspiration that interacts with man's imagination, but has the clear stamp of God's authorship upon it.

I have seen individuals who have experienced similar visions and noted the motivating power of these visions to move people away from worldly fantasy into the realm of godliness.

Nearly 18 years ago a young man, who was a close

friend of mine before I was a Christian, followed me into the family of God one month after my conversion. Like me, before coming to Christ, he had experimented with drugs and Eastern religions. I can still remember the night he surrendered his life to the Lord. He left the church that night with a glowing face that spoke clearly of the work of grace God had done in his heart.

Shortly after that, he shared with me a vision that had been part of his conversion experience. He told me how God had called him to the mission field, and that he had had a vision to go preach the gospel in India. Although I expressed my excitement to him concerning his dream, deep inside was the typical skepticism Christians often have when we meet someone who's young in the Lord and claims to have heard from Him.

Time and my brother's obedience to the heavenly vision were later to prove my doubts wrong. As the years went by, he seemed to move into the ministry with a determination I've seen in few men. Soon, the fruit of his labor began to appear. First, there was a flourishing youth ministry, followed by a successful season as pastor of a large church. It was during this period of expansion that the doors began to open to India's masses. As the years went by, he found himself travelling not only to India to hold large evangelistic crusades, but also to many other nations of the world as doors continued to open for his ministry.

I'll never forget the day we dined together in his home. He had just returned from a large meeting in India. As the tears streamed down his face, he shared with me the joy of watching 150,000 people gather to hear God's Word. He had faithfully preached each night of the crusade and had seen the crowds increase. On the last night, as he turned the meeting over to the nationalist minister who would carry on in his absence, he watched with awe as nearly 75,000 people responded by giving their hearts to Christ.

What began as a tiny seed of vision years earlier had now grown into a reality whose fruit would last forever. His dreams for God's purposes had helped to motivate him from the allurements of the world. The excitement and challenge of evangelism far outshown the glitter of worldly fantasy.

One summer, a few years ago, it was my privilege to sit in a quaint little Mexican restaurant in Kona, Hawaii, and listen to the visions of a man whose dreams had affected a whole generation of young Christians. Loren Cunningham had been our guest for several years at a Christian missions festival I directed. His messages always challenged me. Yet to hear him share personally added a new dimension to the meaning of the word *mission*. God had spoken to Loren at a young age concerning his future. This direction came in the form of a vision.

In a later magazine interview, he shared how God's communication with him was a visual experience. Shutting his eyes on one occasion, he saw the words of Mark 16:15 written in huge block letters. Opening his eyes, the words remained like marble letters to a biblical film epic: GO YE INTO ALL THE WORLD, AND PREACH THE GOSPEL TO EVERY CREATURE.

Years later, the call was expanded through a recurring vision of a world map with waves breaking on distant shores, rolling over continents. Building momentum, the waves continued until they completely covered the land. As Loren came to understand the vision, he saw his mandate to mobilize thousands of youth into missionary endeavors. Over 25 years later, the vision is no longer just a dream.

Youth with a Mission (YWAM), which Loren founded in 1960, has about 20,000 people involved, five thousand of those full-time, long-term missionary workers. Through them, God's Word goes forth from 190 locations around the world. YWAM's 80 missionary training schools prepare the gospel troups that carry the good news into 100 countries each year. Once again, we see the example of God firing a man's imagination with images that bring life and healing to the world.

As exciting as these visions are, they are not without a price. In the 25 years of YWAM's expansion, Loren tells of God's dealings with him andthe heartbreaks that have come his way. Still such crushings do not crush the vision. It seems once a heart is captivated by the heavenly vision, the dream keeps the pilgrim moving on.

Joseph was called a dreamer. His brothers mocked him with the nickname "Dream Master." Still this gentle soul shared the unfolding pictures that flooded into his mind's eye. In his youthful dreams he had seen sheaves bowing before him, the bending stems of grain symbolic of his family. Years later, as he stood with his brothers kneeling at his feet, the vision was fulfilled. At that moment he was not only second ruler of all Egypt, but also God's channel of life that would sustain his loved ones while God formed the foundation from which would rise the mighty nation of Israel. The years of testing and rejection pressed him to his limit and yet the dreamer held on. Godly dreamers who hold on to their dreams will eventually see them fulfilled. When God gives the vision, it *will* eventually come true.

Vision is an essential part of God's economy. The ancient patriarchs followed the inward impressions God gave them like road maps guiding them toward their spiritual destiny. The ancient prophets kept their fingers on the divine pulse and exhorted their countrymen to follow the command of God that funneled through the channel of a sanctified imagination. They understood that vision was an integral part of keeping God's people moving forward.

The Bible says, "Where *there is* no vision, the people perish" (Prov. 29:18). Although it is clear that in this era no "prophet of God" can legitimately claim his words are equal to Scripture, certainly the importance of an inward visual dream, confirmed by Scripture, is a powerful key in moving us toward God's best.

How Do We Dream God's Dream?

Do we merely wait and hope that someday God's dream will pop into our minds? Can Christians do anything to cultivate the soil of the soul into which God can sow His seeds of purpose?

Recently while in Southern California, I rode in a four-wheel-drive truck as it bumped its way over a sprawling 600-acre estate at the edge of Los Angeles. My dear friend John Dawson was giving me a tour of an underdeveloped property for which he was negotiating. His vision was to see the land used as a base for missionary training and world-wide evangelization. He explained to me the plans for the various parts of the property and the practical ways in which he had allowed God to unfold the fulfillment of the vision. His keen obedience to the Lord in the development of this project is perhaps one of the best examples I could use to describe how God releases a vision into our lives.

In the parable of the soils, Jesus explained the dynamics of how the Kingdom of God takes root in a person's life. The story lends itself well to the illustration before us now. God's ideas grow and succeed in the proper soil. One thing I've always admired about my friend has been his openness to creative ideas that come from the Holy Spirit. Good soil is open soil. Broken sod is the best for planting seed.

In the parable, the sower's seed bounced onto the hardened pathway, but failed to take root (see Matt. 13). Even so, a mind closed to the possibility of new ideas will find few sprouting there. True, God does now and then jolt an apostle-Paul type with an uninvited heavenly confrontation. But Paul made it clear in his Epistles the importance of keeping a sensitive heart to the whisperings of the Holy Spirit.

For the last several years, John Dawson walked over the land allowing God to speak to him concerning its potential for His glory. His promptings were not controlled by a presumptuous, greedy longing, but rather the open attitude of allowing God to use the opportunities that crossed his path.

Another quality I've noticed in my friend is his willingness to wait for God's timing. Some of the seed from the sower's hand found its way into soil that restrained its roots from expanding. Someone once wisely stated that the will of God grows on a person. We need to give our visions time to spread out and find the avenues God extends for them. Impatience and presumption can be the stones that limit a vision's growth. Dreams need a solid support system that will bring nourishment to their visible counterparts. Rushing ahead on an impulse may leave behind the opportunity for God to bring along the necessary workers, supporters and counselors.

Perhaps more than any other virtue I've seen in my friend is his determination to keep his motives submitted to God's principles. Selfishness, pride and wrong priorities can choke out a genuine vision before its completion. The seed in the weed-infested soil had only a half-life. A growing vision can become unfruitful when its aim becomes the servant to the personal ambitions of the dreamer.

Keeping the soil of attitude free of thorns will guarantee a healthy crop. Dreamers and visionaries can be a dime-a-dozen commodity in a world looking for subjective thrills, but those who cultivate their spiritual life according to godly injunctions will find their dreams coming true.

As the Bible points out, the worldly visionary will go on building his "towers of Babel." Filthy dreamers will increase as we near the end of our age:

> Likewise also these filthy dreamers defile the flesh, despise dominion, and speak evil of dignities (Jude 8).

> Wisdom *is* in the sight of him who has understanding, but the eyes of a fool *are* on the ends of the earth (Prov. 17:24, *NKJV*).

Godless fantasies will always be a distraction from the disciplines that bring character and virtue. But the godly visionary will find his dreams moving him on. God sustains His dreamers. He keeps their dreams alive, for He desires to make them a reality that will take His love to the very ends of the earth.

TAKING INVENTORY

1. Christians are admonished by God to allow His Spirit to focus our minds on the heavenly dimension, thereby placing us in a position where God can reveal His personal majesty, and His purposes for our lives. Listed below are areas in which Christians need to be active in order to focus in on God's divine plan for our lives:

—In His Word
—In prayer
—In the fellowship of believers
—In activities that edify the Body of Christ

How much time are you currently spending in each of these areas? In what areas do you need to devote more time?

2. We are reminded that God has given special talents and gifts to each of His children. What do you see as God-given talents and gifts in yourself and in your family members? How are you using these gifts to bring glory to God?

10
Stocking Your Armory
Biblical Alternatives

The wonderful thing about submitting our thought life to God is that it allows us to actually step into a new dimension. God doesn't want us to stop dreaming and imagining, He only wants our thinking directed into areas that will be positive and helpful to our Christian growth. Once we decide to close the door to the negative input from the world, we will find ourselves looking for alternatives. Merely shutting our minds to worldly influence is not enough. We must take up the mental weapons that will aid us in resisting the addictive forces of negative imagining.

Stocking Your Armory

This chapter is devoted to providing readers and their families with some of the resources available to counteract the stream of humanistic material that is being offered up today.

It's been estimated that a mere 5 percent of the Christian community makes use of Christian bookstores. As odd as this may seem, many believers are not aware of the vast stock of excellent resources offered by these businesses. In recent years the Christian book and Bible industry has gone through some major changes. The tiny stores of the past, with limited inventory and poor locations, are being replaced by modern and well-stocked retail outlets that offer many excellent aids for spiritual growth. This vast resource is left untapped by much of the Body of Christ.

Contemporary Christian Music

Even as David's harp playing soothed a troubled King Saul, so there are modern-day Davids who have learned how to effectively bring God's message into the turmoil of our modern world. Perhaps more than any other field of Christian endeavor, the field of contemporary Christian music offers the most promise, as well as potential for the greatest amount of controversy.

In an attempt to relate to the changing culture of twentieth-century America, many Christian artists have adopted styles that are up-to-date with many that are found among secular performers. Their approach often works, giving the listener a clear biblical message, along with a musical quality and excellence that is on a par with any contemporary performance.

Some artists, however, in pursuing the goal of being relevant, have tossed out biblical guidelines and are wandering into questionable territory. Therefore, as we approach this area I recommend that we study the variety of musical options available and then readers should prayerfully decide what will be best for them and their families.

I've listed some of the more popular musical artists presently on the Christian market. Listed are the names of the particular performers or groups, their predominant style and the age group to which they generally appeal:

FEMALE VOCALISTS

NAME	STYLE	AGE
Sandi Patti	Traditional	18-Adult
Debbie Boone	Pop-Rock	15-30
Cynthia Clawson	Variety	18-Adult
Nancy Honeytree	Light Rock	18-35
Karen Kelly	Variety	18-Adult
Twila Paris	Pop	15-30

MALE VOCALISTS

Steve Green	Variety	18-Adult
Phil Driscoll	Variety	12-Adult
Michael W. Smith	Pop-Rock	12-30
Larnelle Harris	Variety	18-Adult
Russ Taff	Pop-Rock	18-35
Carmen	Variety	13-25
Wayne Watson	Pop	18-30
Keith Green	Light-Rock	20-40
Steve Camp	Pop-Rock	15-30

GROUPS

Bill Gaither Trio	Variety	18-Adult
Silverwind	Pop-Rock	13-Adult
Imperials	Variety	18-Adult
Mylon LeFevre	Rock	15-35
2nd Chapter of Acts	Pop-Rock	18-35
Dallas Holm	Light Rock	18-35
Degarmo and Key	Pop-Rock	15-30

CHILDREN'S RECORDS

Music Machine	Variety	2-12
Bullfrogs and Butterflies	Variety	2-12
Animals and Other Things	Variety	2-12
Kids Praise I-V	Variety	2-12
Kids Sing Praise	Variety	2-12

Guidelines for Selecting Listening Material

For the discerning listener I suggest following biblical guidelines in selecting suitable listening material. Some Christians feel that contemporary Christian music is amoral.

I don't. And although I don't feel that one musical style is demonic and another divine (i.e., rock versus classical), Christians do need to be discerning as to what builds up our spiritual being and what does not.

It's my personal conviction that Christian musicians have similar responsibilities to those of a minister. Frequently these individuals have greater input into our lives than pastors and evangelists. The frequency with which we listen to them and the emotional avenues their music opens in us allow them an almost intimate access to our inner lives. Therefore I recommend using the following principles when deciding what you will expose yourself to.

First of all, we need to ask, what is the message? What are the lyrics saying? Some of the words can be deeply moving, with strong scriptural truth that encourage us toward more positive Christian virtues. Others can be trite, cynical, and at times, even unbiblical. Simply because the lyricist has strung his words together nicely does not mean they will edify us. I'm grateful that today there are many Christian musicians who have strong and clear messages.

Second, we should ask what are the methods used in putting across the musical message? Musicians have the sort of nature that is unique and often misunderstood by those of a different temperament. God uses their sensitivity to reflect the variety of His creative resources. It's this wonderful expressive talent that moves and inspires us. It's also for this very reason that when artistry is used as licence for excess, the listener can be carried into compromise. Once again, righteous judgment (see John 7:24) is necessary in making a selection of what we will or will not expose ourselves to.

Many musicians have blended their musical gifts with a joyous, triumphant and poignant performance that stirs up in us godly desire. Others have allowed different forces to

135

come into play and have polluted the stream. Put simply, they have used sensual or sexual styles rather than wholesome celebration.

We would do well to ask ourselves if the performance exalts the performer rather than the Saviour. When the apostles Paul and Barnabas brought the miraculous power of the gospel to Lystra, a man who had been crippled from birth was healed. The local population was so impressed that they attempted to worship the gospel messengers. Paul and his companion clearly restrained their ardent fans, being careful to give God the glory for the healing (see Acts 14:15-17). Some contemporary religious performers are unaware of this scriptural guideline, or simply choose to ignore it.

As much as we appreciate the messengers, we must remember that they are only human and if their message or methods fall short of godly principles, we need to remove their influence from our lives and humbly pray that God will show them how to properly represent His Kingdom.

The Christian View of Sexuality

Not all that has come out of the sexual revolution of the 1960s is negative. Because of the increased awareness of sexuality, there is now an openness to discuss this whole issue.

There have always been problems with promiscuity and sexual perversion. And although the increased access to illicit materials has helped to multiply this problem in recent years, ignorance about sex isn't bliss.

Many Christian leaders and counselors have pointed out that one of the best ways of guaranteeing that the sexual problems are handled properly is to deal with them openly and honestly. We are blessed with a wealth of materials today that deal with these problems from a biblical perspective and are available from many reliable sources.

Another positive factor in this area are the breakthroughs that concerned groups have been making on the frontlines of the war against pornography. Recent declines in the circulation of major "skin" magazines are no doubt the result of concerted efforts of these groups. *Playboy* and *Penthouse* magazines have seen their circulation fall by nearly 3 million and 1 million, respectively.[1]

Recent efforts by groups protesting the sale of pornography in convenience stores have resulted in one chain, 7-Eleven, removing sexually explicit materials from their stores' inventory.[2] Although only stores directly owned by the parent corporation, Southland Corp., were ordered to do this, the feeling is that the other related franchises will follow suit.

Another chain, Thrifty Drug and Discount Stores, banned the sales of *Playboy, Penthouse* and *Playgirl* magazines in all of their 582 stores in the West.[3]

A recent statement by the Attorney General's Commission on Pornography, showing the relationship between sexually violent and degrading pornography and violence toward women, is another blow against this perverted industry.[4] Still the commission's opponents are determined to refute the statement and such determination plainly shows that the battle is far from over. Prayer and protest seem to be powerful tools that are turning the tide in this war.

We can rejoice that these triumphs have been won and that there will be more to follow. But another realm where the standard needs to be kept high is in the homes and lives of individual Christians. Balanced and thoroughly researched books on the subject of sexuality offer strong resources to the individuals seeking to help themselves and their families.

Listed are just a few of the dozens of excellent resources on the subject of sexuality available for youth and adults:

> *Dating, Sex and Friendship* by Joyce Huggett/Inter-Varsity Press.
> *Running the Red Lights* by Charles Mylander/Regal Books.
> *Sex and the Single Christian* by Barry Colman/Regal Books.
> *Tough Questions About Sex* by Dawson McAllister/Word (Video).

Honest and compassionate discussion, along with correct knowledge concerning problems in this area is the best solution to improper sexual fantasies.

Christian Videos

It's been estimated that 40 percent of homes in America have VCRs.[5] This fact is disheartening as well as encouraging. On the one hand, Americans, teenagers included, will have greater access to sexually explicit and violent films. But on the other hand, if the Christian media industry is quick to respond, they can invade this tremendous new market with films that offer positive alternatives. With the VCR, families have the capability of controlling and increasing the selection of entertainment they watch on TV.

Recent surveys have shown that 85 percent of Christian videos now being rented are being rented by individuals.[6] For those looking to substitute the present deluge of fantasy with positive Christian movies, the opportunities are greater than ever. The following is a listing of just some of what's offered on the market through many local Christian bookstores:

Elementary School-age Children

Cross Currents (dramatic, action-packed) 30 min., message oriented.

Gingerbrook Fare 1 (clowns, fun) teaches obedience, 40 min.

Great Banana Pie Caper (dramatic, humorous) 28 min., message oriented.

Mountain Lady (dramatic) 59 min., message oriented.

Mystery of Willowby Castle (dramatic) 30 min., message oriented.

The Goosehill Gang (action/adventure) Series of four, 40 min. each.

Wolfhunter (dramatic) 34 min., message oriented.

The Greatest Adventure: Stories from the Bible/Hanna Barbera:

David and Goliath
Daniel and the Lion's Den
Noah's Ark
Joshua and the Battle of Jericho
Moses
Samson and Delilah

Youth (Teens)

The Belonging Game (amusing/realistic drama) 30 min.

The Dating Movie (drama/real-life interviews) 46 min.

139

Eighteen (dramatic story/teenage life) 52 min.

Football Fever (pro bloopers/testimonies) 40 min.

Jill (dramatic story/teenage/cancer) 30 min.

Run to the Sea (action packed/dramatic) 55 min.

Adults

Greater Than Gold (drama/family pressures) 63 min.

A Father, a Son, a Three-Mile Run (drama/family) 65 min.

Sand Castles (drama/family life) 80 min.

Christian Adventure Literature

One area in the Christian's stockpile of positive alternatives is the area of Christian literature. With the increasing lack of literacy among Americans, adults and youth alike those who spend time reading good Christian literature will not only enrich their lives spiritually, but also keep their mental processes alive as well.

Besides the Bible, Christian biographies are some of the best reading available today. These true stories are not only exciting, but faith building as well. I'm sure many of today's Christian leaders can look back to the tremendous influence stories of outstanding missionaries or heroes of the faith have had on their own lives. I've listed below just a handful from among the hundreds of books available along this line:

Run Baby, Run by Nicky Cruz and Jamie Buckingham/Jove.

Codeword Catherine by Jodie Collins/
Tyndale.

The Hiding Place by Corrie tenBoom and
John Sherrill/Bantam.

Joni by Joni Eareckson and Joe Musser/
Bantam.

God's Smuggler by Brother Andrew/Spire.

Is That Really You, God? by Loren
Cunningham/Chosen.

The Boy Who Sailed 'Round the World Alone
by Robin Graham/Word.

Christian Fiction Books

Although these stories come from the realm of imagination, those who dream them up are fine, godly authors with something powerful to say through this channel of communication. This area of lighter reading is one that all of us need from time to time to break up the hectic pace of our lives in this busy age. It's a privilege to have such a wide variety of titles and subjects to pick from. Youth and children can be especially benefited by the interesting stories that creative Christian authors offer on today's Christian market. A list of just a few of the many books available follows:

Youth Fiction (preteens)

The Peppermint Gang Series by Laurie B.
Clifford/Tyndale.

Sugar Creek Gang Series by Paul Hutchens/
Moody/Ages 8-10.

What If Books by Laurie B. Clifford/Regal/
Ages 10-12.

Books for Guys (teens)

John, Son of Thunder by Ellen Gunderson Traylor/Tyndale.

Captive Planet by Catherine McGuire/Random.

Baker Street Series by Terrance Dicks/Lodestar.

My Brother, My Enemy by George Bishop/Nelson.

Books for Gals (teens)

Heartsong Books:

Anne by Muriel Canfield/Bethany.
Carrie by Carole Page/Bethany.

Springflower Books:

Erica by Eileen Pollinger/Bethany.
Jill by Mary Carraway/Bethany.

Francena Arnold Series/Moody

Not My Will
Then Am I Strong
The Road Winds On.

Biblical Novels by Lois T. Henderson/Harper and Row:

Abigail
Hagar
Lydia
Miriam

Adult Fiction (Women)

George MacDonald Series, Michael R. Phillips (editor)/Bethany:
The Fisherman's Lady
The Marquis' Secret
The Musician's Quest.

Others:

When Breaks the Dawn by Janette Oke/Bethany.
The Wishing Star by Marian Wells/Bethany.
Two from Galilee by Marjorie Holmes/Revell.
Three from Galilee by Marjorie Holmes/Harper and Row.

Reading for Men
Space Trilogy by C.S. Lewis/Macmillan.
Holy War by John Bunyan/Baker.
My Brother, My Enemy by George Bishop/Nelson.
The Roman Solution by Wallace Henley/Tyndale.
Holy Fool by Harold Fickett/Good News.
Warning by George Hirthler/Inter-Varsity Press.
John, Son of Thunder by Ellen Gunderson Traylor/Tyndale.

Toys

As we mentioned in an earlier chapter, toys have great potential to influence young, impressionable minds. Offering options for our offspring is extremely important in an era when more and more sophisticated types of toys are tied to themes that are unbiblical.

It's only been recently that Christian organizations have

jumped into this field in a serious way. Companies like We Win Toys market several lines of children's playthings with biblical tie-ins. There is one line with characters based on heroes of the Bible that children can place in different poses. There's also a line of stuffed animals and dolls representing godly principles. Another group that has jumped into this field in a serious way is Praise Unlimited. This company offers dolls and other products aimed at giving children positive biblical alternatives.

One organization dedicated to producing quality products based on biblical principles is Anthony Paul. Directed by Tony Salerno, the founder of Agape Force, many of the company's staff are responsible for the creation of a number of popular children's recordings, including *Music Machine* and *Bullfrogs and Butterflies*. This talented staff has now begun developing toys. Their first major concept, Pleasant Dreams®, will be available in both the Christian and general markets, fall of 1986.

Pleasant Dreams® incorporates cuddly stuffed animals made of calico and storybooks/cassettes. Like the parables Jesus used to teach the multitudes, Pleasant Dreams'® stories use everyday experiences and feelings as a foundation to teach children biblical principles and high moral standards in ways they will understand and enjoy.

The stories are set in the Land of Pleasant, a beautiful place children can visit only when they are asleep and dreaming. In the stories, the calico animals come to life and take their child visitors on exciting adventures/lessons that involve both characters, but focus on the growth of one. Impatient children see the need for patience; high-speed dogs see the need to slow down; and insecure characters learn self-worth.

It's exciting to see groups like these attempting to counteract the wave of destructive playthings that have inundated our culture. The future leaders of the Church are our little ones. Providing them with materials that will inspire them to know and follow God is a major part of raising a godly generation. I trust that the suggestions I've made in this brief overview will be useful in guiding you in your own investigation into positive alternatives to the Fantasy Explosion.

It's been said many times that when God takes something damaging out of our lives He always replaces it with something better. In the spiritual realm we are delivered from the power of darkness and translated into the Kingdom of God (see Col. 1:13). Darkness is exchanged for light. The old gives way to the new. So it should be in the realm of our thought life. God is not interested in merely erasing the tape of our dreams and leaving it blank. He wants us to develop the God-given capacity for creative thinking.

Imagination is part of our lives. Studies have shown that fantasizing is part of learning.[7] Dreamers are builders. Visionaries helped establish this country and open up the frontiers of science and technology. Edison, Ford and Bell, their names speak volumes. These were all men with dreams, constructive dreams.

In the field of the arts, much of which the Church has abdicated to the world, we have what seems an endless opportunity to use our talents for God in creative ways. If we are to invade the field of communication with God's message, we need to be training a generation of creative, godly thinkers who can display the kind of excellence in the arts and media that will glorify God and communicate the truth with the quality it deserves.

In recent years, the Church has rallied behind the call to change our culture by bringing the principles of righteousness back into government. Protests against pornography and abortion have seen results. All of these efforts are an important part of what it means to let our light shine before men. The city that is set on the hill will not only be appreciated for the strength of its walls and the thickness of its gates, but also for the beauty of its architecture.

Architects are dreamers and the greatest one of all is the God who created substance, grace and beauty from nothing. Surely we have the opportunity to join with Him and, in our own limited human realm, create and proclaim ideas that come from pure minds illuminated by God's Word.

If you have children who are tugged at by the deviant fantasies of the world perhaps its because they are sensitive and talented individuals who also are being swayed by the technical or artistic excellence of these productions. One approach for guiding them away from these false images is to challenge them to use their talents for God.

Talk with your children about the fantasies facing this generation. Help them to see through the deceptions that confront them. Offer them alternatives. Try looking at their situation in creative ways and ask God to give you answers that will compel them to higher things. Provide the alternatives we have mentioned and find others to augment them.

If you are personally struggling in any of the areas we have talked about, take these guidelines to heart. Offer yourself alternatives. Pursue the godly options that are made available through church programs, interesting books and, most of all, prayer and stimulating study of Scripture. Today there are more godly alternatives available for Christians than ever before. Fixing your mind on the good and pure is possible. Churches, Christian media (TV and radio) and Christian bookstores all provide a vast stockpile of positive information with which we can fill our hearts, minds and lives.

The choice is ours. God will help us overcome. He's promised that no temptation is too great (see I Cor. 10:13). A mind filled with God's Word is a mind that can dream. Who knows what great things will come to those who chose to dream God's dream and have the courage to trust Him to bring those dreams to pass.

TAKING INVENTORY

1. The author suggests that Christians need to seek positive alternatives to the negative influences coming our way via the world. List some of the positive alternatives you and your family are already pursuing either individually or collectively. What are other areas you would like to look into?

2. Readers are encouraged to ask themselves two questions when choosing contemporary Christian music: (a) What is the message? and (b) What methods are being used in putting across the musical message? How do these questions relate to other areas of the media?

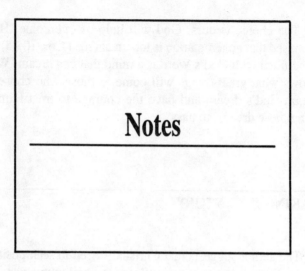

Notes

Preface

1. "Close Encounters on Photon," *Newsweek*, July 23, 1984, p. 62.
2. "Whodunit?," *Life*, Nov. 1984, p.109.
3. "Databank," *Fantastic Films*, Jan. 1985, p. 13.

Chapter 1

1. "Neo-Nazis Using Ex-professor's Novel as Guide for Violence," *Sacramento Bee*, Dec. 30, 1984.
2. Gregor T. Goethals, *The TV Ritual: Worship at the Video Altar,* (Boston: Beacon Press, 1981), p. 2.
3. Robert Reinhold, "Overwhelming Violence—TV Time," *New York Times*, May 6, 1982.

Chapter 2

1. Kandy Strand, "My Turn," *Newsweek*, May 6, 1985.
2. Reported by one youth pastor who attended the concert as a concerned observer.
3. David Gergen, "X-Rated Records," *U.S. News and World Report*, May 20, 1985, p. 98.
4. "Parents Vs. Rock," *People*, Sept. 16, 1985, pp. 46-51.
5. "Rock Is a Four-Letter Word," *Time*, Sept. 30, 1985, p. 70.
6. "See You in Hell," © Ebony Ltd., 1983, 1984.
7. *Sacramento Bee*, April 11, 1985.
8. "Motley Crue Speak Out," *Hit Parader*, March 1985, p. 54.

9. Ibid., p. 52.

10. "White Noise, How Heavy Metal Rules," *The Village Voice*, Arts, June 18, 1985, p. 48.

11. Bob Greene, "Words of Love," *Esquire*, May 1984, pp. 12, 13.

12. Patrick Goldstein, "Want Your Children 'Demented'? Call Greg, Pop Eye," *Los Angeles Times*, June 16, 1985, p. 86.

13. Ibid.

14. Russ Kazal, "Will Teenagers Emulate Their Idol, Madonna, and Bare All?" *Sacramento Bee*, July 12, 1985.

15. Judith Reisman, United Press International.

16. "How Muzak Manipulates You," *Science Digest*, May 1984.

17. "Women in a Video Cage," *Newsweek*, March 4, 1985, p. 54.

18. "Sing a Song of Seeing," *Time*, Dec. 26, 1983, p. 56.

19. Ibid., p. 55.

20. Veronica Young, "Rock Music Videos," *Horizon International*, Mar.-Apr. 1984, pp. 12, 15.

21. "Sing a Song of Seeing," *Time*, Dec. 26, 1983, p. 63.

22. Young, "Rock Music Videos."

23. "Women in a Video Cage," p. 54.

24. Dan Sperling, "Mixed Feelings on Video Violence, the Cruelty of Motley Crue," *U.S.A. Today*.

25. "Women in a Video Cage," p. 54.

26. Ibid.

27. "Symbols Link Night Stalker Suspect with Satanism," *Tacoma News Tribune*, Sept. 2, 1985.

28. "'Stalker' Suspect Pleads Innocent, Hails Satan," *Sacramento Bee*, Oct. 25 1985.

Chapter 3

1. Lynn Hirschberg, "Giving Good Phone," *Rolling Stone Yearbook, 1983*, p. 141.

2. Ibid.

3. "The Porno Plague," *Time*, April 5, 1976, p. 58.

4. Ibid.

5. Peter Bogdonovitch, *The Killing of the Unicorn*, (New York: Morrow, 1984), pp. 15, 16.

6. Paul A. Tanner, "How to Wage War on Porn," *Charisma*, May 1985, p. 73.

7. "New Themes and Old Taboos," *Newsweek*, March 18, 1985, p. 67.

8. Ibid.

9. *National Federation of Decency Journal*, Oct. 1985, p. 16.

10. "This Isn't Shakespeare," *Newsweek*, March 18, 1985, p. 62.

11. Martin Mawyer, *Moral Majority Report*, Aug. 1985, p. 3.

12. Ibid.

13. *Newsweek,* March 18, 1985, p. 61.

14. Mawyer, *Moral Majority Report.*

15. "And Animal House Begat . . . ," *Time,* April 15, 1985, p. 103.

16. Jim Burns and Carol Bostrom, *Handling Your Hormones,* (Laguna Hills, CA: Merit Books, 1984).

17. Daniel Goleman, "Sex Fantasies," *Sacramento Bee,* March 8, 1984, p. 3.

18. Ibid.

19. Ibid.

20. "The Porno Plague," *Time,* April 5, 1976, p. 62.

21. Tom Minnery, "What It Takes to Fight Pornography," *Advance,* Oct. 1985, p. 8.

22. Christian Update, *Christian Herald,* July/Aug. 1985, p. 4.

23. "At a Glance," *Pentecostal Evangel,* Dec. 9, 1984, p. 27.

24. "Sexual Violence in the Media," *Psychology Today,* Jan. 1984, p. 14.

25. Ibid.

26. "Deadly Fantasies Spurred Killers, FBI Study Says," *Tacoma News Tribune,* Sept. 26, 1985, p2.

27. *National Federation of Decency Journal,* p. 11.

28. Ibid., p. 8.

29. Bob Greene, "Girlfriend Shed It All," *Sacramento Bee,* March 21, 1984, p. AA2.

30. Mawyer, *Moral Majority Report,* p. 4.

Chapter 4

1. "The Occult Blossoms into Big Business," *U.S. News and World Report,* Nov. 7, 1983, p. 83

2. Ibid.

3. *Newsweek,* July 23, 1984.

4. Ibid.

5. Phil Wiswell, Video Worlds, *Omni,* Jan. 1984, p. 58.

6. Ibid., p. 100.

7. "Campus Game Nearly Fatal," *San Francisco Chronicle,* Dec. 14, 1981, p. 2.

8. *Survival Sports News,* Sacramento, CA, p. 2.

9. John Skow, *People,* Oct. 24, 1983, p. 44.

10. "School Kids Spice Up LIfe with Play Dope," *Sacramento Union,* Feb. 23, 1985.

11. Dungeons and Dragons® Tract, Jesus People U.S.A. Reprinted by permission, *Cornerstone,* 4707 N. Malden, Chicago, IL 60640.

12. Player's Handbook, p. 20, par. 4.

13. Dungeon Masters Guide, p. 42.

14. Deities and Demigods Instruction Manual, p. 5, par. 3.

15. *Cornerstone,* Dec. 1980.

16. *Psychology Today,* Nov. 1980.

17. Dungeon Masters Guide, p. 31.
18. Ibid., p. 75.
19. Deities and Demigods, p. 35.
20. Moira Johnson, "It's Only a Game—Or Is It?" *New West,* Aug. 1980, p. 38.
21. John Eric Holmes, "Confessions of a Dungeon Master," *Psychology Today,* Nov. 1980.
22. Player's Handbook, pp. 192, 220.
23. *Rolling Stone,* Oct. 1980.
24. *International Herald Tribune,* Aug. 16, 1983.
25. Johnson, "It's Only a Dream"Or Is It?" p. 38.
26. *Life,* March 1982.
27. *Imagination: Gift of God,* Phillips Ministries, P.O. Box 901874, Dallas, TX 75390-1874.
28. Albert James Dager, "Playing with Danger," *Media Spotlight,* 1985.
29. Ibid.
30. *Imagination: Gift of God.*
31. "Toying with Kids TV," *Newsweek,* May 13, 1985, p. 85.
32. Ibid.
33. Ibid.
34. Dager, "Playing with Danger."
35. J. Isamu Yamamoto, "The Quest for Power," *Spiritual Counterfeits Newletter,* Sept. 1983, p. 8.
36. Benjamin Demott, "Darkness at the Mall," *Psychology Today,* Feb. 1984, p. 48.
37. Yamamoto, "The Quest for Power," p. 9.
38. Demott, "Darkness at the Mall," p. 50.
39. Ibid.
40. Yamamoto, "The Quest for Power," p. 9.
41. Demott, "Darkness at the Mall," p. 50.

Chapter 5
1. *Los Angeles Times,* June 16, 1985.
2. Woodrow Nichols, "Star Wars and the Film Company," *The Pergamum 5th Column,* Fall 1979.
3. *Newsweek,* May 19, 1980, p. 73.
4. *Rolling Stone,* July 24, 1980, p. 37.
5. Ibid., p. 37.
6. C.S. Lewis, *The Screwtape Letters,* (Old Tappan, NJ: Fleming Revell, 1978).
7. *Time,* Nov. 7, 1977, p. 105.
8. A Directory of Religious Bodies in the U.S., (Garland, 1977).
9. "Battlestar Galactica and the New Mythology," *His,* May 1979.
10. *Sacramento Bee,* Oct. 12, 1980.

11. Lynda Hurst, *Toronto Star,* Sec. D, June 13, 1981.

12. *Los Angeles Times,* June 16, 1985.

13. *Rocky Mountain News,* People, Sept. 27, 1982.

14. Arthur C. Clarke, *Childhood's End,* (New York: Ballantine, 1953).

Chapter 6

1. "Adults, Not Kids, Are the TV Couch Potatoes," *U.S.A. Today,* Aug. 28, 1983, p. 123.

2. "Tube Boobs of the World, Unite!", *People,* Dec. 12, 1983, p. 123.

3. Marilynn Preston, "Who's Afraid of the Big Bad Box?", *U.S.A. Today,* July 1, 1985, p. 53.

4. Richard Cohen, "The Cohen Column," *Sacramento Bee,* May 28, 1984.

5. "They're Puttin' on the Glitz," *Time,* Nov. 5, 1985, p. 76.

6. Ibid., p. 77.

7. Cyra McFadden, "Soaps as Therapy," *Panorama,* Jan. 1981, p. 5.

8. "At a Glance," *Pentecostal Evangel,* Feb. 17, 1985.

9. N. Katzman, "TV Soap Operas: What's Going on Anyway?", *Public Opinion Quarterly, 36,* 1972.

10. Velma Angel, *Those Sensational Soaps,* (Brea, CA: Uplift Books, 1983). Used by permission.

11. Kenrick and Gutierres, 1980.

12. Angel, *Those Senational Soaps.*

13. "What Entertainers Are Doing to Your Kids," *U.S. News and World Report,* Oct. 28, 1985, p. 48.

14. Angel, "Those Sensational Soaps."

15. *National Federation of Decency Journal.*

16. George Gerbner and Larry Gross, "The Scary World of TV's Heavy Viewer," *Psychology Today,* Apr. 1976, p. 44.

17. Mary Ann Grossman, "Worlds Apart," *Sacramento Union,* Sept. 19, 1984, pp. G-1 and G-8.

18. Ibid., p. G-8.

19. Ibid.

20. Ibid.

Chapter 7

1. *Sacramento Bee,* Jan. 25, 1984.

Chapter 8

1. "What Entertainers Are Doing to Your Kids," *U.S. News and World Report,* Oct. 28, 1985, p. 46.

2. "Calvin Meets the Marlboro Man," *Time,* Oct. 21, 1985, p. 69.

Chapter 10

1. *The Church Around the World*, Vol. 16, No. 4, Tyndale

2. Jim McLain, "Sex Magazines Banned from Chain's Racks," *Ventura County Star Free Press*, May 4, 1986.

3. Ibid.

4. "Naughty Photos," *Time*, May 26, 1986, p. 27.

5. Will Tusher, *Variety*, May 14, 1986, p. 19.

6. Pat Robinson, "Video Update," *Booksellers Journal*, May 1986, p. 121.

7. "Cross Talk," *Psychology Today*, Apr. 1985, p. 22.

Fantasy Explosion

☐ **Video** ☐

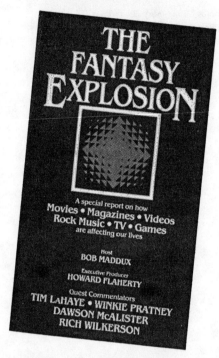

A documentary on videocassette, also entitled *Fantasy Explosion,* examines the role fantasy plays in our culture today. It is specially produced for use with youth groups, parents and leaders, and may be rented or purchased by calling Gospel Light Video, toll-free (800) 235-3415 (outside CA), (800) 227-4025 (inside CA), or check with your local Christian bookstore.